Towards a Wor

The OCR An

Conflict – the Student Guide

David Wheeler

Red Axe Books

ISBN: 978-1911477044

Find us at

www.dogstailbooks.co.uk

CONTENTS

Introduction

I hope you find this revision guide useful. It consists of an individual analysis of each poem in the OCR Anthology – *Towards a World Unknown* - with the cluster of poems entitled Conflict. The analysis of each poem follows the same pattern: there is a section on the poet and the context in which the poem was written and some facts about each author; unfamiliar words are explained; and then each poem has a commentary which focuses on both what the poem is about and the style, form and structure that the poet uses. A final section on each poem summarizes the poem's overall impact and effect. There are no colours, few illustrations, but you will get a clear sense of what each poem is about and each poem's overall effect.

Who or what is this book for?

Perhaps you missed that crucial lesson on one particular poem that you find hard to understand? Good lessons are better than this book, because through different activities and through careful questioning and probing your teacher will help you to arrive at an understanding, an appreciation of the poem that you work out for yourself – and that process is invaluable – it's a process of thinking and exploring as a group, in a pair perhaps and as an individual, and, no matter how good the notes that your class-mates made, those notes are no substitute for having been there and gone through the process of the lesson. So, maybe, through absence, you feel a little out of touch with some of the poems: this book will help you.

Alternatively, you may want to read about ideas which you have not encountered in class. On the other hand, you may have the sort of teacher who allows you to respond in your own way to the poems; that is a completely valid and worthwhile approach, of course, but it does not suit every student: some students like to have clear guidelines about the meaning of what they read and to have various interpretations suggested to them so that they are at least aware of the overall gist of the poem. It still leaves you free to make up your own mind and have your own ideas, but it does provide a starting point – this book will give you that starting point.

You may be trying to revise the poems in the final days and weeks before the exam and want a quick refresher on poems that you first studied in class a long time ago; maybe it was a Friday afternoon and you weren't paying complete attention; maybe you were late for the lesson and never quite 'got' what the poem is about; maybe you were distracted by something more interesting happening outside and spent the lesson gazing out of the window. This book will help you get to grips with those poems.

It is very unlikely, but you may be reading these poems on your own for the very first time – this book will help you too, because I have assumed that you know nothing about the poem or about poetry, and the commentary on each poem is written so that you can start from scratch. Of course, some of you might find this a tiny bit condescending – and I apologize for that. I should also apologize if there are ideas in this book which are different from ones you have encountered before in class. There are as many different ways to read a poem as there are readers, and each reader might have a slightly different view of a particular poem – as we shall see. For example, most readers (pupils, teachers, professional critics) would agree that 'London' by William Blake is critical of the society he lives in; most would agree that 'London' is a bitter attack on the London that he lived in, but quite what the final verse means is open to a variety of interpretations!

So... if you want a book that tells you what each poem means; comments on features of style and structure; suggests the tone or the overall impact of each poem; gives you the necessary background knowledge to understand each poem – then this is it. At the end you will find a glossary of poetic terms, but after this introduction, there is a commentary on each poem – each commentary is self-contained and can be read on its own. Throughout the book I have used the words that I would use if I were teaching a lesson on these poems – if I use words you don't know or haven't heard, then look them up. Part of education, part of writing well about Literature is the way you yourself write, so to expand your vocabulary is a good thing. Terms which have specific literary meanings are all in the glossary at the back of the book.

Help Yourself!

I hope you find this book helpful in some ways, perhaps many ways. It deliberately does not include very detailed information about the authors for two reasons. Firstly, it would be a waste of space. Secondly, the internet is a rich source of information about writers and their work – an internet search on any of your studied poets or poems will throw up all sorts of interesting resources, including student chat boards, online revision chat-rooms as well as more obvious sources of information like Wikipedia or web sites associated with a particular author. Where there is detailed biographical information here, it is because it is vital to an understanding of the poem.

But do be warned – all the information you can possibly find about a particular poet may help to clarify something you already sensed about the poem, but it is no substitute for engagement with the poem itself. And in the examination the examiner does <u>not</u> want to read a potted biography of the poet whose poem you have chosen to write about. Besides - generalizing from what we know about a writer or his/her era is a dangerous thing: for example, it is important to be aware of William Blake's political beliefs and to be aware that he wrote 'London' during the years of the French Revolution – some might say that without such an awareness the poem cannot be fully appreciated and understood – BUT that will not help you explain the impact of individual words and lines and images at all, nor will it help you write well in the examination. Very often I have started my commentary on a poem with necessary information to help you understand it, but you don't need to reproduce all that information in the exam - it is there to help you fully understand significant details about the poem; to try to reproduce the process of discovery that a good lesson will guide you through. But it probably has little place in the examination.

You may be the sort of student who is doing English Language or English Literature because it is compulsory at your school. But it may also be that as you progress through the course you come to feel that English is a subject that you like and are good at; you may even be intrigued or fascinated by some of the poems in the anthology. If that happens, then do not rely on this book. Look on the internet for resources that will further your interest. For example, if one poet makes a special impact on you – read some of their other work; you will find a lot of it available on-line. Many of the poets in the Literary Heritage sections are now out of copyright – their work is freely available on-line. Many of the contemporary poets have their own websites which can be a fascinating source of extra information and contain links to other poems or biographical information. So there are many ways in which you can help yourself: it's a good habit to get into, especially if you start thinking about the possibility of doing English at A level.

But please remember this is no substitute for a close engagement with the poems themselves. And just as importantly – this book is no substitute for a good lesson which allows you to think about the poem's language and ideas, and then slowly come to an understanding of it. After understanding it (and that is an emotional as much as a logical understanding of it), you may come to appreciate it. What does that mean? Well, as you go through the course and read more and more poems then you may find that you prefer some to others. The next step is to identify why you prefer some poems to others: in this there are no right answers, but there are answers which are clearer and better expressed than others. And preference must be based on reasons to do with the way the poem is written or its overall emotional impact: it's your job to put what you think and feel into words – I cannot help you do that. I can merely point out some of the important features and meanings of the poems. As you grow in confidence and perhaps read other writing on these poems or listening to your teacher or your classmates, then you will start to formulate your own opinions – stealing an idea from one person, a thought from somewhere else and combining all these different things into your own view of the poem. And that is appreciation. As soon as you say you prefer one poem to another you are engaging in a critical reaction to what you have read – in exactly the same way that people prefer one film to another or one song or performer to another.

Romanticism

In this cluster of poems the first three are designated Romantic poems and it is important that you have an understanding of what Romanticism was. It has very little to do with the word 'romantic' as we apply it today to an event like Valentine's Day.

Romanticism is the name given to the artistic, political and cultural movement that emerged in England and Germany in the 1790s and in the rest of Europe in the 1820s and beyond. It was a movement that saw great changes in literature, painting, sculpture, architecture and music, and found its catalyst in the new philosophical ideas of Jean Jacques Rousseau and Thomas Paine, and in response to the American, French and industrial revolutions. Its chief emphasis was on freedom of individual self-expression, sincerity, spontaneity and originality, but it also looked to the distant past of the Middle Ages for some of its inspiration. In Romantic thought the nature of the poet changed: no longer was a poet someone who could manipulate words well and with skill; the poet was a special individual with a unique vision to communicate and with special insights to communicate through his poetry.

The key characteristics of Romantic poetry in English are:

- a reverence for and veneration of the natural world.

- a belief that the poet was a special person who had important truths to communicate and whose experiences were more intense than those of ordinary people.

- an emphasis on individualism and intense emotion.

- a increased interest in ordinary people – the rural poor and the urban working classes.

- a political radicalism, best summed up by the watchwords of the French Revolution – liberty, fraternity, equality.

- an overwhelming emphasis on the sensibility and imagination of the poet.

- an interest in medieval and ancient history.

- a veneration of Shakespeare.

- a desire to be original and to reject the orthodoxies of the immediate past.

Of course, not all the poets that we label 'Romantic' displayed all these characteristics all through their careers.

Contemporary Poetry & the Literary Heritage

You will probably have noticed that the poems within each section or cluster of your anthology are designated as Literary Heritage poems. Why? Contemporary poetry consists of poems written in the very recent past by living poets and they are here because as you study English or English Literature, it is felt to be important that you realize that poetry is not dead and poetry is not only written by dead white Englishmen: it is alive and it is being written now all over the English-speaking world by men and by women from a wide variety of backgrounds. So the contemporary poems are there to remind you that poetry is alive and well and thriving. Indeed, as I have already mentioned, many of the contemporary poets have their own websites or perform poetry readings which you may be lucky enough to attend during your course. You can also see some performances of these poems on the internet.

The poems in the first half of the anthology are generally by dead white Englishmen, although there are some poems by women. That sounds dismissive (dead white Englishmen), but it's not meant to be. They are in the anthology to remind you that writers have been writing poetry in English for hundreds of years and that what happens over those centuries is that an agreement emerges about which poems are some of the greatest or most significant ever written in the English Language. How does such agreement emerge? Well, mainly through people continuing to read the poems, responding to them and enjoying them; another concrete way is for the poems to appear in anthologies – which ensures them an even wider audience. The point you need to grasp is that writing in English poetry has been going on for hundreds of years and what has been written in the past influences what is written now. Many contemporary poets will have read the poems that you will read in the Literary Heritage sections. So when you read, for example, 'Ozymandias' by Percy Shelley for the first time, you will be joining the millions of English-speaking people all over the world who have read and enjoyed that sonnet. Organizations like the BBC have also run public votes where members of the public can vote for their favourite poem – another way that we know which poems are popular. Such poems then become part of the canon. That is not to say, however, that there is only agreement about the value of poems from the distant past: some like those by Seamus Heaney and Ted Hughes are from the closing decades of the 20th century; they are included because already there is widespread agreement that these poets are important and influential and that their poems are rewarding to read and study and enjoy.

So part of our heritage, part of the culture of speaking English, whether you speak English in Delhi or London or Manchester or Lahore or Trinidad or Liverpool or Auckland or Toronto or Cape

Town or Chicago, is centuries of English poetry and a continuing poetic culture which is rich and vibrant, and includes voices from all over the English-speaking world.

The Secret of Poetry

The secret of poetry, of course, is that there is no secret. Nonetheless, I have come across lots of students who find poetry challenging or off-putting or who don't like it for some reason. I find this attitude bizarre for all sorts of reasons. But some students are very wary of poetry or turned off by it. If you are – rest assured: you shouldn't be!

Poetry is all around us: in proverbial sayings, in popular music, in the nursery rhymes we listen to or sing as children, in playground skipping chants, even in the chanting heard at football matches. All these things use the basic elements of poetry: rhythm and rhyming and very often the techniques of poetry – alliteration, repetition, word play. Advertisements and newspaper headlines also use these techniques to make what they say memorable. Ordinary everyday speech is full of poetry: if you say that something is 'as cheap as chips' you are using alliteration and a simile; if you think someone is 'two sandwiches short of a picnic', if someone is 'a pain in the arse', then you are using metaphors – the only difference is that when poets use similes and metaphors they try to use ones that are fresh and original – and memorable, in the same away that a nursery rhyme or your favourite song lyrics are memorable. Even brand names or shop names use some of the techniques of poetry: if you have a Kwik Fit exhaust supplier in your town you should note the word-play (the mis-spelling of Kwik) and the assonance – the repetition of the 'i' sound. There must be several hundred ladies' hairdressers in the UK called 'Curl Up and Dye' – which is comic word-play. You may go to 'Fat Face' because you like what they sell, but I hope that when you go next time, you'll spare a thought for the alliteration and assonance in the shop's name.

Poets also play with words. So when students tell me they don't like poetry, I don't believe them – I feel they have simply not approached it in the right way. Or perhaps not seen the link between the poetry of everyday life and the poetry they have to study and analyse for GCSE.

Poetry has been around a very long time: the earliest surviving literature in Europe consists of poetry. As far as we can tell poetry existed even before writing, and so poems were passed down by word of mouth for centuries before anyone bothered to write them down. If something is going to be passed down and remembered in this way, then it has to be memorable. And, as we shall see, poets use various techniques and tricks and patterns to make what they write easy to remember or striking in some way - just as you may remember the words to your favourite song or to a nursery rhyme that was recited to you as a small child. Let us take one example. The opening sentence of Charles Dickens' novel *A Tale of Two Cities* is

It was the best of times; it was the worst of times.

It is not poetry, but it is very memorable, because Dickens uses simple repetition, parallelism and paradox to create a very memorable sentence. Parallelism because the two halves of the sentence are the same – except for one word; and paradox because the two words – best and worst – seem to contradict each other. Now look at this recent slogan from an advert for Jaguar cars:

Don't dream it. Drive it.

This uses the same techniques as Dickens: parallelism and paradox (or juxtaposition) and it also uses alliteration. It is all about manipulating words to give them greater impact – to make them memorable.

As I am sure I will repeat elsewhere, it is always vital to read a poem aloud: your teacher might do it very well, you might be lucky enough to hear one of the living poets in the anthology read their poems aloud or you can access many recordings via the internet. I think reading a poem aloud is a good way to revise it: it has been claimed that when we read something aloud we are reading twenty times slower than when we read with our eyes – and that slowness is vital, because it allows the sound of the poem, the turn of each phrase and the rhythm of each poem to stand out. As we shall see, the way a poem sounds is absolutely crucial to its impact – for one thing, it helps you pick out techniques such as alliteration and assonance.

One of the things we will discover is that poetry is partly about pattern – patterns of sounds, of words, of rhythm; patterns of lay-out too, so that a poem and the way it is set out on the page - often separated into separate stanzas (don't call them verses) – is vital. If you quickly glance at a page from the anthology, you would probably assume that what is on the page is a poem – because we have certain expectations of the way that poems look. So what? You have probably been aware for a long time that poets often organize what they write into stanzas. For me this an absolutely crucial part of poetry because as human beings we are in love with patterns, we are addicted to patterns – and that is one of the many reasons we love poetry or find it so appealing. Patterns dominate our lives. We may have patterns on our clothes, our furnishings, our curtains, our carpets. But patterns rule our lives more completely than that: seen from above even a housing estate has patterns – the street lights at regular intervals, the garages and gardens in the same relationship to the houses; a spider's web on a frosty morning; the unique patterns of snowflakes; a honeycomb; your school uniform perhaps; the rhythm of your day, of the timetable you follow at school, of your week, of the seasons and of the year. And where patterns do not exist we like to invent them: the periodic table of elements (which you may be familiar with from Chemistry) does not exist as a table out there in nature – it's the human need to organize and give things a pattern which is responsible for the way it looks. Or look at a map of the world, criss-crossed by lines of longitude and latitude – and invented by the human mind as an aid for navigation.

What on earth has this to do with poetry? Well, poetry, especially from the past, likes to follow patterns and this structure that poets choose is something we instinctively like; it is also important when poets set up a pattern, only to break it to make whatever they are saying even more memorable because it breaks the pattern. We will see this happen in some of the poems in the anthology.

Let us look at it another way. Take the sonnet: if you choose to write a sonnet, you are committing yourself to trying to say what you want to say in 140 syllables, arranged in equal lines of 10 syllables each and fitted to a complex rhyming scheme. It is very hard to do, so why bother? Partly because it is a challenge – to force you to condense what you want to say into 140 syllables concentrates the mind and, more importantly, makes for language that can be very condensed and full of meaning. And, of course, the sonnet has been around for centuries so to choose to write one now means you are following (and hoping to bring something new and surprising) to a long-established form.

So what is poetry? *The Oxford Concise Dictionary of Literary Terms* defines it as:

Language sung, chanted, spoken, or written according to some pattern of recurrence that emphasizes the relationships between words on the basis of sound as well as sense: this pattern is almost always a rhythm or metre, which may be supplemented by rhyme or alliteration or both. All cultures have their poetry, using it for various purposes from sacred ritual to obscene insult, but it is generally employed in those utterances and writings that call for heightened intensity of emotion, dignity of expression, or subtlety of meditation. Poetry is valued for combining pleasures of sound with freshness of ideas....

Remember some of these phrases as you read this book or as you read the poems in the Anthology – which poems have intensity of emotion? Are there some which have a freshness of ideas? Or do some make you think about things more deeply (subtlety of meditation)? Perhaps there are poems which make you do all three? What can I possibly add to the Oxford Book of Literary Terms? Think of your favourite song – whatever type of music you listen to. The song's lyrics will share many of the characteristics of poetry, but the words will be enhanced by the music and the delivery of the vocalist. Is it a song that makes you happy or sad? Angry or mellow? Whatever it makes you feel, a song takes you on an emotional journey – and that is what poems do too, except they lack musical accompaniment. So think of a poem as being like a song – designed to make you feel a particular emotion and think particular thoughts; like some songs, the emotions, the thoughts, may be quiet complex and hard to explain but the similarity is there. And that is another reason why it is important to hear the poems read aloud – they are designed to be listened to, not simply read. Short poems like the ones in the Anthology are often called lyric poems – and that is because hundreds of years ago they would have been accompanied by music. Before 1066 Anglo-Saxon bards telling even long narrative poems used to accompany themselves on a lyre – a primitive type of guitar and up to modern times lyric poems have been set to music and performed.

Making Connections

As you can see from what is written above, a lot of the work in English on the Anthology is about making connections – the exam question will explicitly ask you to do this. As you study the Anthology or read this book you should try to make connections for yourself. Free your mind and make unusual connections. You might feel that some poems take you on a similar emotional journey; some poems might use metaphor or personification in similar ways; some poems were written at the same time as others and are connected by their context.

If you can connect poems because of their written style or something like structure or technique, then that will impress the examiner more than if you simply connect them by subject matter. The poems are already connected by simply being in the Anthology, so to start an answer, for example, by stating that two poems are about 'Conflict' is a waste of words. You should try to do some thinking for yourself as you read this book and reflect on the poems in the anthology– because it is a good habit to get into and helps prepare you mentally for the exam.

Do you have a favourite word? If you do, you might like to think about why you like it so much. It may well have something to do with the meaning, but it might also have something to do with the sound. Of course, some words are clearly onomatopoeic like *smash*, *bang* and *crack*. But other words have sound qualities too which alter the way we react to them – and they are not obviously onomatopoeic. For example, the word *blister* sounds quite harsh because the letter *b* and the combination of *st* sound a little unpleasant; and, of course, we know what a *blister* is and it is not a pleasant thing. On the other hand, words like *fearful* or *gentle* or *lightly* have a lighter, more delicate sound because of the letters from which they are made. Words like *glitter* and *glisten* cannot be onomatopoeic: onomatopoeia is all about imitating the sound that something makes and *glitter* and *glisten* refer to visual phenomena, but the *gl* at the start and the *st* and *tt* in the middle of the words make them sound entirely appropriate, just right, don't they?

Think of it another way: just reflect on the number of swear words or derogatory terms in English which start with *b* or *p*: *bloody, bugger, bastard, plonker, pratt, prick, prawn* – the list goes on and on. The hard *c* sound in a word like *cackle* is also unpleasant to the ear. So what? Well, as you read poems try to be aware of this, because poets often choose light, gentle sounds to create a gentle atmosphere: listen to the sounds. Of course, the meaning of the word is the dominant element that we respond to, but listen to it as well.

You don't need to know anything about the history of the English language to get a good grade at GCSE. However, where our language comes from makes English unique. English was not spoken in the British Isles until about 450 CE when tribes from what is now Holland invaded as the Roman Empire gradually collapsed. The language these tribes spoke is now known as Old English – if you were to see some it would look very foreign to your eyes, but it is where our basic vocabulary comes from. A survey once picked out the hundred words that are most used in written English: ninety-nine of them had their roots in Old English; the other one was derived from French. The French the Normans spoke had developed from Latin and so when we look at English vocabulary – all the words that are in the dictionary – we can make a simple distinction between words that come from Old English and words that come from Latin – either directly from Latin or from Latin through French. [I am ignoring for the moment all the hundreds of thousands of words English has adopted from all the other languages in the world.]

So what? I hear you think. Well, just as the sounds of words have different qualities, so do the words derived from Old English and from Latin. Words that are Old English in origin are short, blunt and down-to-earth; words derived from Latin or from Latin through French are generally longer and sound more formal. Take a simple example: house, residence, domicile. *House* comes from Old English; *residence* from Latin through French and *domicile* direct from Latin. Of course, if you invited your friends round to your residence, they would probably think you were sounding rather fancy – but that is the whole point. We associate words of Latinate origin with formality and elegance and sometimes poets might use words conscious of the power and associations that they have. Where a poet has used largely Latinate vocabulary it creates a special effect and there are poems in the Anthology where I have pointed this feature out. Equally, the down to earth simplicity of words of English origin can be robust and strong.

Alliteration is a technique that is easy to recognize and is used by many poets and writers to foreground their work. It can exist, of course, in any language. However, it seems to have appealed to writers in English for many centuries. Before 1066 when the Normans invaded and introduced French customs and culture, poetry was widely written in a language we now call Old English, or Anglo Saxon. Old English poetry did not rhyme. How was it patterned then? Each line had roughly the same number of syllables, but what was more important was that each line had three or four words that alliterated. Alliterative poetry continued to be written in English until the 14th century and if you look at these phrases drawn from everyday English speech I think you can see that it has a power even today: busy as a bee, cool as a cucumber, good as gold, right as rain, cheap as chips, dead as a doornail, kith and kin, hearth and home, spick and span, hale and hearty. Alliteration can also be found in invented names. Shops: Coffee Corner, Sushi Station, Caribou Coffee, Circuit City. Fictional characters: Peter Pan, Severus Snape, Donald Duck, Mickey Mouse, Nicholas Nickleby, Humbert Humbert, King Kong, Peppa Pig. The titles of films and novels: *Pride and Prejudice, Sense and Sensibility, Debbie Does Dallas, House on Haunted Hill, Gilmour Girls, V for Vendetta, A Christmas Carol, As Good as it Gets, The Witches of Whitby, The Wolf of Wall Street.* Alliteration is an easy way to make words and phrases memorable.`

So what? Well, as you read the poems and see alliteration being used, I think it is helpful to bear in mind that alliteration is not some specialized poetic technique, but is part of the fabric of everyday English too and it is used in everyday English for the same reasons that it is used by poets – to make the words more memorable.

An Approach to Poetry

This next bit may only be relevant if you are studying the poems for the first time and it is an approach that I use in the classroom. It works well and helps students get their bearing when they first encounter a poem. These are the Five Ws. They are not my idea, but I use them in the classroom all the time. They are simply five questions which are a starting point, a way of getting into the poem and a method of approaching an understanding of it. With some poems some of the answers to the questions are more important than others; with some poems these questions and our answers to them will not get us very far at all – but it is where we will start. I will follow this model with each commentary. They are also a good way to approach the unseen poem. The five questions to ask of each poem you read are:

- Who?

- When?

- Where?

- What?

- Why?

WHO? Who is in the poem? Whose voice the poem uses? This is the first and most basic question. In many poems the poet speaks as themselves, but sometimes they are ventriloquists – they pretend to be someone else. So first of all we must identify the voice of the poem. We must ask ourselves to whom the poem is addressed. It isn't always right to say – the reader; some poems are addressed to a particular individual. And, of course, there may well be other people mentioned in the poem itself. Some poetry is quite cryptic, so who 'you' and 'they' are in a poem make a crucial difference to the way we interpret it. Why are poems 'cryptic'? Well, one reason is that they use language in a very compressed way – compressed perhaps because of the length of each line or the decision to use rhyme.

WHEN? When was the poem written and when is it set? This is where context is important. We know our context: we are reading the poem now, but when the poem was written and when the poem is set (not always the same, by any means) is crucial to the way we interpret it. The gender or background of the poet might be important, the society they were living in, the circumstances which led them to write the poem – all these things can be crucial to how we interpret the poem.

WHERE? Where is the poem set? Where do the events described in the poem take place? With some poems this question is irrelevant; with others it is absolutely vital – it all depends on the poem. In the Anthology you will find some poems which depend on some understanding of where they are set for them to work; you will find other poems where the location is not specified or is irrelevant or generalized – again it depends on the poem.

WHAT? This means what happens in a poem. Some poems describe a place; some describe a particular moment in time; some tell a story; some have a story buried beneath their surface; some make statements – some may do several or all of these things at once. They are all potentially different, but what happens is something very basic and should be grasped before you can move on to really appreciate a poem. Very often I have kept this section really short, because it is only when you start to look closely at language that you fully understand what is going on.

WHY? This is the hardest question of all and the one with a variety of possible answers, depending on your exact view of the poem in question. I like to think of it as asking ourselves 'Why did the poet write this poem?' Or 'What is the overall message or emotional impact of this poem?' To answer it with every poem, we need to look at all the other questions, the way the poet uses language and its effect on us, and try to put into words the tone of the voice of the poem and the poem's overall impact. Students in the classroom often seem puzzled by my asking them to discuss the poem's tone. But it boils down to this - if you were reading the poem out loud, what tone of voice would you use? What is the mood or atmosphere of the poem? Does the poet, or whoever the poet is pretending to be, have a particular attitude to what he or she is writing about? Answering these questions helps us discuss the tone of the poem. But you may not agree with everybody else about this and this is good: through disagreement and discussion, our understanding of what we read is sharpened. In the commentaries on each poem in this Anthology this question 'Why?' is answered at the very end of each commentary, because it is only after looking closely at the poet's use of language, form and structure that we can begin to answer it. If you feel you know the poem well enough, you might just use the section 'Why?' for each poem as a quick reminder of what its main message is. For all the poems the 'Why?' section consists of a series of bullet points which attempt to give you the words to express what the poem's main point is.

A Word of Warning

This book and the commentaries on individual poems that follow are full of words to do with literature – the technical devices such as metaphor, simile, oxymoron. These are the vocabulary to do with the craft of writing and it is important that you understand them and can use them with confidence. It is the same as using the word *osmosis* in Biology or *isosceles* in Maths. However, in the examination, it is absolutely pointless to pick out a technique unless you can say something vaguely intelligent about its effect – the effect is vital! The examiner will know when a poet is using alliteration and does not need you to point it out; the sort of writing about poetry that consists of picking out technical devices and saying nothing about their effect or linking them in some meaningful way to the subject matter is worthless. I will suggest, in each commentary, what the effect might be, but we can generalize and say that all techniques with words are about making the poem memorable in some away – and this 'making something memorable' is also about foregrounding language. Language that is foregrounded means that it is different from normal everyday language and that it draws attention to itself by being different – it would be like if we all went round every day and tried to use a metaphor and alliteration in everything that we said or if we tried speaking in rhyme all day – people would notice!

Warming Up

Before we look at any of the poems from the anthology, I want to briefly examine four poems to give you a taste of the approach that will be followed throughout the rest of the book. So we will start by looking at four completely different poems. All of which are based on conflict. I am going to subject the poems to a full analysis and I will demonstrate with the four poems some crucial ways of reading poetry and give you some general guidance which will stand you in good stead when we deal with the poems in the anthology itself. This is not meant to confuse you, but to help. I cannot stress enough that these four poems are not ones that you will be assessed on. They are my choice – and I would use the same method in the classroom – introducing a class very slowly to poetry and 'warming up' for the anthology by practising the sorts of reading skills which will help with any poem. Besides, you may find the method valuable in your preparation for answering on the unseen poem in the exam.

The first poem we will consider was written during the First World War by Wilfred Owen., whose poem 'Anthem for Doomed Youth' is in the Anthology. This poem is called 'Futility':

Move him into the sun -
Gently its touch awoke him once,
At home, whispering of fields unsown.
Always it woke him, even in France,
Until this morning and this snow.
If anything might rouse him now
The kind old sun will know.
Think how it wakes the seeds, -
Woke, once, the clays of a cold star.
Are limbs, so dear-achieved, are sides,
Full-nerved - still warm - too hard to stir?
Was it for this the clay grew tall?
- O what made fatuous sunbeams toil
To break earth's sleep at all?

Context

Wilfred Owen (1893 – 1918) is widely regarded as the leading British poet of the First World War. He died in action on November 4th 1918 – just seven days before the war finally came to an end. Owen was an officer and was awarded the Military Cross for leadership and bravery in October 1918. The shock of what he saw in the front-line moved him to produce a great many poems in a very short time – most of which were not published until after his death. He seems to have been particularly keen to ensure that the British public was told the horrific truth about the war. He developed his own use of half-rhyme which was to influence other poets for the whole of the 20th century.

'Futility' is one of only five poems that were published when Owen was alive. It was published in a magazine called *The Nation* in June 1918. The compassion that Owen reveals in this poem for the suffering of the ordinary soldier is typical of his work; some of his other poems though, are more brutal and horrific in their realism.

Owen was one of many British writers who felt moved to describe what they saw of the war in the trenches of France and Belgium – and it is a subject to which British writers have returned again and again.

Why? Most people would agree that all wars are horrific and cause death and terrible injuries, so what was it about the First World War that so captures the imagination of generation after generation of writers? It seems that the First World War was unique because it caused huge numbers of deaths on all sides without any obvious effect on the course of the war; infantry troops were sent from their trenches to almost certain death and battles lasted for months with only a tiny movement of the front-line – so there was huge loss of life with no clear objective: it began to seem pointless to those involved in it and that pointlessness is echoed by this poem's title. Added to that, the conditions in the trenches – where the men lived and fought and often died – were appalling.

Futility – uselessness.

the clay – humanity. In the Bible God creates man from a lump of clay.

fatuous – foolish

Who? Owen speaks as himself.

When? In the present – *this morning, this snow*. But we know from the biographical context that this poem is set during the First World War – the poem itself contains no military detail at all.

Where? From the poem we know it is set in France; from our knowledge of Owen, we know that this is set in the trenches of the front-line.

What? A soldier has died. The speaker wants to move him into the sun, since that surely will bring him back to life. It doesn't - and the speaker reflects on the sadness and pity of the death as well as thinking about the bigger questions of human existence.

Commentary

The poem begins with an order - *Move him into the sun* - perhaps given by an officer. A soldier has died in the night – frozen to death in the snow it seems. In a sense, *how* he has died is irrelevant – it is the fact that he has died that Owen finds so shocking. He comes from the countryside and has always woken at dawn – *whispering of fields unsown* suggests that in Britain he worked on the land and had to sow seeds in fields, but this might also suggest the promise for the future growth that seeds contain. Because the sun had always woken him and had woken him *gently*, the speaker articulates an innocent trust that the *kind old sun* will wake him now. But, of course, it won't. The tone of this opening stanza is gentle with soft sounds; even the personified sun used to whisper to the young man.

The second stanza begins by pointing out that our solar system and our planet only exists because of the sun. Owen ends the stanza with three questions that simply cannot be answered without calling into doubt any religious faith and our very existence. Human beings are seen as the summit of evolution – *so dear achieved* – but the poet wonders why Creation occurred at all, if it will end in tragic deaths like this one: the sunbeams that helped create life on earth are *fatuous* and powerless. And this makes Owen question the whole point of human existence. Here in the second stanza the rhythm is broken up by the dashes and question marks which give a faltering, uncertain mood to the poem. Is Owen bitter or simply puzzled and confused about why we are here on this planet?

This is a very memorable poem in all sorts of ways. It uses half-rhyme to suggest that something very profound is wrong with what Owen describes, but it has no specific references to the First World War – apart from the word *France*. This perhaps gives the poem a timeless quality – it could apply to all deaths in all wars and the sense of futility that Owen feels could be applied to every death of a young person. It fits the definition of freshness of ideas because Owen uses one individual death to question the very nature of our existence on earth, the point of human existence and the nature of God – and he does so in only 12 lines – a remarkable feat of compression. This is a poem that is not just anti-war – it is also, one might say, anti-God because it questions why we are on earth if all that is going to happen is that we will die. It is a tender, poignant and gentle poem, full of a profound sadness at the thought of anyone dying before their time. Nature is important in the poem too: the dead soldier is at home in nature and at ease with the rhythms of nature but that does not help him escape death.

Why?

This short gentle poem raises important issues:

- Life on earth seems pointless when we are faced with the death, especially of young people.

- The sun (which might be symbolic of God as the creator of the planet) can create a whole world, but cannot bring one young man back to life.

- What is the purpose of human life on earth? The poet cannot accept that it is to kill each other in war.

- God – given the questions in the second stanza – seems not to exist or at least not to care about individual human deaths.

Here is the second poem that we will look at as an unseen:

The Sick Rose by William Blake

O rose, thou art sick!
  The invisible worm,
That flies in the night,
  In the howling storm,

Has found out thy bed   5
  Of crimson joy,
And his dark secret love
  Does thy life destroy

thou – you

thy - your

Who? The voice of the poet, the invisible worm, a rose.

When? In the night during a storm.

Where? Hard to say... in the bed of the rose.

What? Just using what we know from the poem, we can say that an invisible worm discovers the dark secret love of the rose and destroys it during a storm.

It is obvious that this method will not get us very far with this type of poem or, at least, will not get us beyond a superficial interpretation of what it means. Before you read any further, please take the time to read my comments below about William Blake's poem 'London' on page 40, because Blake is also the author of 'The Sick Rose'.

What can we say with any certainty about this poem? Its mood is sinister. It is night-time and there is a howling storm. An invisible worm has found out where the rose has its bed and is coming to take its life. *Found out* suggests that the bed needs to be hidden. Paradoxically, although the worm is going to destroy the life of the rose, the worm has a *dark secret love* for the rose: this is now especially disturbing – a love which is dark and secret and which is destructive of life. Not only is it night and, therefore, dark, but the love of the worm is also dark and secret and destructive. We expect love to be a positive emotion which brings good things to our lives.

When faced with this poem many readers want to interpret the poem symbolically – otherwise it becomes a poem about horticulture. The poem is full of words that we associate with love - *rose, bed, joy, love*. In addition, in our culture sending someone roses, especially red roses, is a token of love. But this is a love which has gone wrong and is destructive. Many readers also find the shape of the worm rather phallic – suggestive of the penis. Think of all the types of love which might be considered 'wrong' or destructive. This is the list I came up with, but I am sure you can think of many others:

- Love for someone who does not love you back.

- Love for someone who is already married or in a relationship.

- Love which cannot be expressed.

- Love that transmits disease through unprotected sex.

- Love between two people from different religions.

- Love which is against the law.

- Love which is unwanted by the person you love.

- Love between two people of different class backgrounds.

- Love between two people of the same gender.

- Love or sexual expressions of love which are condemned by the church or by religious doctrine or law.

- Love which is possessive and selfish.

The point of this list is really to show that Blake's power of compression suggests a love that has gone wrong and leaves us to interpret it. To say that 'The Sick Rose' is about any one of the situations listed above would be totally wrong; to say that it suggests them all and encompasses them all, suggests the power of Blake's writing.

If you have read 'London' and if you remember that the rose is the national symbol of England, then this poem becomes even more than a poem about love gone wrong – it becomes (perhaps) a poem about the state of England and a warning that it will soon be destroyed. You don't have to identify exactly what or who the worm is – the poem does that for you: the worm is destructive and capable of killing – it is a symbol of ALL the things Blake hated in his society. Blake's point is that the rose is sick and is about to be destroyed by sinister, invisible powers.

Finally, if you need any proof of Blake's power to compress meaning, just look at how many words I have used in an attempt to give meaning to his words: Blake uses (including the title) only thirty-seven! This is part of the poem's power and art – that is uses powerful words and imagery from which we can extract a multitude of meanings.

Why? This astonishingly compressed and darkly evocative poem is

- a protest about the England that Blake lived in.

   a protest about the way the church and society saw certain types of love as wrong.

- a warning that love – or what we call love- can be destructive if it is not fulfilled.

- a plea for tolerance and inclusion for those who conventional morality condemns.

We will examine two more poems which deal with conflict as part of the introduction. The first is called 'Belfast Confetti' and was written about the fairly recent troubles in Ireland.

'Belfast Confetti' – Ciaran Carson

Context

Carson was born in Belfast in 1948 and has lived there all his life. Violence and its effects are central to much of his writing – he has lived throughout the 'Troubles' - the name given to the last forty years of the history of Northern Ireland. During the Troubles terrorist groups representing both sides of the conflict attacked each other and the British Army, and planted bombs which deliberately targeted civilians too. This poem was written in 1990, but the term 'Belfast confetti' was already in use in speech and means the shrapnel (pieces of metal) placed around explosives that would fly out and injure people when the explosive was detonated or it can mean random objects made of heavy metal which rioters hurled at the soldiers or the police during riots.

There has been violence in Ireland ever since the English tried to conquer it and make it a colony in the 16th century. The most recent era of violence is known as the Troubles and flared up in the late 1960s. Tension between Catholic and Protestant communities erupted into violence and British troops were sent to Northern Ireland to keep the peace, to keep the opposing sides apart. However, because of various factors, the violence escalated and terrorist groups on both sides of the sectarian divide became involved and increasingly powerful. There were many deaths and many bombings, and the violence continued into the late 1990s. Carson was brought up in the Falls Road area – one of the most dangerous areas of Belfast.

It is dangerous to generalize about Ireland, but essentially the Catholic community favoured unification with the Republic of Ireland, while the Protestant community wanted to remain as part of the United Kingdom. More immediately, in the 1960s the Catholic community did not have equal rights because the Protestant majority dominated politics. The British government claimed the British soldiers were in Northern Ireland to keep the peace, but Irish Republicans felt they were an army of occupation

fount – this word means two things in this poem. It is a spring of water like a fountain, but it is also a fount of broken type: before computers, books and newspapers were printed using metal blocks to represent each letter and piece of punctuation which were laboriously put in position by hand. These metal blocks are not unlike the pieces of metal used as shrapnel.

Balaklava, Raglan, Inkerman, Odessa, Crimea – street names in the Falls Road area which ironically recall the Crimean War – another British imperial war, you might argue. You can read more about the Crimean War in the section devoted to *The Charge of the Light Brigade* by Alfred Tennyson.

Saracen – a British army armoured personnel carrier.

Kremlin-2 mesh – a type of mesh used over the windows of Saracens and designed to protect the windows from bombs and rockets.

Makrolon face-shields – Makrolon is a tough man-made substance which protects the face but is transparent.

fusillade – a continuous discharge of guns.

Who? The poet speaks as himself.

When? During the Troubles.

Where? In the Falls Road area of Belfast.

What? The poet is caught on the streets of Belfast when a bomb is detonated. He seems to get lost in the confusion and chaos after the explosion and describes the British Army's own confused reaction to the incident.

Commentary

This is a confused and confusing poem which you may struggle to make sense of – but it is deliberately written in this way to suggest that this sort of incident is frightening and confusing and it also demonstrates the inability of language to describe adequately what is going on. The title of the poem *Belfast Confetti* is an everyday, darkly-comic term for shrapnel or for odd pieces of metal thrown at the British soldiers during riots: it is a euphemistic slang term and derives its comic edge from our usual association of confetti with weddings which are happy, joyous occasions – unlike the riot described in this poem. It becomes darkly comic because we normally associate confetti with weddings not bombings. The 'confetti' - the shrapnel - rains down on the streets of Belfast once the bomb has exploded, and continues as the rioters use odd scraps of metal to bombard the British soldiers.

In the first stanza the poet struggles to make sense of what is going on. He is caught up in a riot and then a bomb explodes, adding to the confusion. The very first word – *suddenly* – plunges us into the midst of the action. In the wake of the explosion the air is *raining exclamation marks*: this metaphor suggests the pieces of shrapnel flying through the air; the shouts and cries of people near the bomb's blast; and also the sheer sense of shock and fear that courses through the poet. Carson continues this metaphor of the shrapnel as pieces of punctuation to suggest that language and its tools – punctuation – cannot make sense of, or convey the reality of, the riot and the bomb. *This hyphenated line* becomes *a burst of rapid fire*. The poet tries to formulate a sentence in his head, but he cannot complete it – his sense of fear and panic and shock is so strong that he has lost the ability to communicate. To make matters worse, at the end of the stanza he cannot escape – everywhere is *blocked with stops and colons*.

In the second stanza the poet is lost in his home area. The tense switches to the present to give extra immediacy. He knows *this labyrinth so well*, but cannot escape. The list of street names adds to his sense of confusion. As I have already mentioned the names are highly ironic since they are named after places in the Crimea where the British Army fought; except Raglan Street which is named after Lord Raglan, the British army commander-in-chief during the Crimean War. Everywhere he finds a dead-end. The short sentences echo his confusion and also give us the sense that he is trying to move quickly in order to get off the streets to the safety of his home. Line 15 is full of references to British soldiers, but they are described in terms of their equipment – in a list like the street names – which makes them seem dehumanized and threatening. The soldiers are not presented as human and in line 16 they fire a series of questions at him – a *fusillade of question marks*. *Fusillade* is a brilliantly chosen metaphor which is appropriate since the soldiers are asking the questions, but also suggests how potentially dangerous these questions seem to the poet in his state of panic:

My name? Where am I coming from? Where am I going?

Clearly the soldiers are trying to catch the bombers and these are genuine questions which they might have asked someone running in the streets in the aftermath of a riot and a bombing, but they are more important than that. In fact, the whole poem (composed of two stanzas of equal length) is an extended metaphor which suggests that conflict destroys language and our ability to communicate normally: 'raining exclamation marks' suggests rapid shouts of fear and alarm; 'an asterisk on the map' would look like there had been an explosion on the paper; 'stuttering' obviously shows the poet cannot get his words out because of his fear, but also suggests the sound of the 'rapid burst of fire'; the alleyways are 'blocked with stops' just as full stops block the reader at the end of the sentence.; a fusillade refers to several questions being fired at the narrator but also means rapid gunfire.

Carson's sense of total disorientation, his fear and total confusion, mean that he is unsure of who he is and where he's going, so great has been his sense of shock.

Conflict

The poem enacts the conflict of the riot situation very effectively through language, the disrupted rhythm and the extended metaphor. The British soldiers are dehumanized and it is easy to see them as an army of occupation – certainly their brief interrogation of the poet causes conflict. This conflict is internalized as the poet panics and is desperate to get to the safety of his home.

Why? This poem

- uses lists, questions and short, unfinished sentences to convey an atmosphere of fear and chaos.

- shows no overt interest in the political situation, but is wholly concerned with the reactions of one frightened and confused man.

- suggests, it could be argued, through its presentation of the soldiers and the careful selection of street names which recall foreign wars, that the British Army is an army of occupation.

- uses language to suggest the inability of language to adequately convey the reality of a riot and a subsequent bomb blast.

- enacts through its language and imagery the extreme sense of shock and disorientation that the poet feels.

Our final poem also comes from a recent conflict – the text of the poem is readily available online.

'Invasion' – Choman Hardi

Author

Choman Hardi is Kurdish and was born in 1974. Her family moved to Iran in 1975 and returned to Iraq in 1979. They had to flee Iraq in 1988 when Saddam Hussein started attacking the Kurds with chemical weapons. In 1993 she came to Britain as a refugee and is now a poet, translator and painter. She had collections of her poetry published in Kurdish before she started writing in English. This poem is autobiographical; the border is the border between Iran and Iraq. This poem was published in 2004 in the collection *Life for Us*.

Context

The story of the Kurdish people is a sad one. The Kurds have their own language, culture and traditions which stretch back thousands of years, but they live in five different countries: Turkey, Iraq, Iran, Syria and Armenia. So they exist as a people, an ethnic group, but they do not have their own country. Because they are a minority in the different countries in which they live, they have often been persecuted for being different and because they want to have more political independence in the countries in which they live. Because of this, many Kurds have gone into exile in order to escape persecution and oppression. Ideally, I suppose, they would want their own country, Kurdistan, which unites all the Kurdish people, but that is very unlikely to happen, because it would mean other countries giving up territory. In recent times they have suffered most persecution in Iraq under the rule of Saddam Hussein.

You may feel you need to know a little about recent Iraqi history to fully understand the context of this poem. Saddam Hussein became the President of Iraq in 1979 and in 1980 started a war with neighbouring Iran. Iran had just had an Islamic Revolution and presumably Saddam Hussein thought he could benefit Iraq by waging war against an unstable neighbour. The war ended in 1988 and caused hundreds of thousands of deaths. During the war the loyalty of the Iraqi Kurds was called into question and they were attacked by Saddam's own troops – it is this attack which the poem seems to be based upon, but Saddam mounted frequent attacks to suppress and kill the Kurdish population.

In 1990 Iraq invaded Kuwait and the First Gulf War began in 1991: a mainly British and American army forced the Iraqis out of Kuwait; once again Saddam's regime used the Kurds as a scapegoat for the national failure and many Kurds escaped from Iraq into neighbouring Turkey. In 2003 a British and American army invaded Iraq and toppled Saddam from power. Iraq has been a troubled country ever since, but the Kurds in the north of Iraq do now have a measure of autonomy within the state of Iraq in a region known as Kurdistan.

Who? The narrator is a Kurd awaiting an attack by the Iraqi army. The future tense is used throughout the poem to give a building sense of apprehension and fear. The attack is inevitable, as is the defeat and deaths of the villagers, faced with a fully-equipped army.

When? Not specified but likely to be in the late 1980s or the early 1990s. After the First Gulf War of 1991, after his defeat, Saddam Hussein sent his army north to attack the Kurds.

Where? In the area of northern Iraq known as Kurdistan.

What? The narrator – who uses 'we' to speak for the whole community - awaits with fear and apprehension the forthcoming attack and the violence that will erupt.

The opening sentence *Soon they will come* gives a feeling of tension, especially as *they* are nor identified or named; *soon* suggests something sudden and the future tense underlines that it is inevitable. The waiting narrator and the rest of her village will hear *the sound of their boots* before they *appear through the mist*. The enjambment in the first stanza suggests an unstoppable force, the lines sweeping forward just as the advancing troops will do. Dawn can sometimes be a time of hope, but here it brings an attacking army which can be heard before they emerge from the mist.

Their attackers are further dehumanized by being described as wearing *death-bringing uniforms* – they have come not to control the village, but to kill the people in it and destroy their houses. The conflict is highlighted by the poet's use of *we* for her community and *they* for the soldiers. Enjambment is used in this verse too to suggest the forward advance of the attacking troops. 'Death-bringing' is a fresh and original compound adjective.

The third stanza asserts that the enemy will meet resistance from *young men/with rusty guns and boiling blood*. The fact that the guns are rusty indicates that the young men cannot fight on equal terms with the enemy who also have tanks, and we have the first mention of blood which foreshadows the future for the village and the fourth verse of the poem. The young men's blood is 'boiling' with anger at this unprovoked attack on their homes and families. *Boiling blood* alliterates and is juxtaposed with *rusty guns* – this is not an equal fight, which underlines the inevitability of the bloodshed to come. The sense of an entire community under threat is emphasized by the fact that the fighters are *our young men* whose *short-lived freedom* is about to end in a brutal way.

The fourth stanza starts with the stark and short statement – *We will lose this war* – where once again the use of the future tense stresses the inevitability of defeat. The defeat will have a profound physical and psychological effect on the community:

>...*blood*
>*will cover our roads, mix with our*
>*drinking water, it will creep into our dreams.*

The positioning of *blood* and *dreams* at the end of their respective lines highlights the way the attack and the shedding of blood will traumatize the people of the Kurdish community. Note that the poet uses triadic structure in this verse by picking out three things that the blood will do - the first two physical, the last one mental and emotional. *Creeping into our dreams* suggests very forcefully the appalling psychological effects this unprovoked attack will engender: they are being attacked only because of who they are.

The final stanza gives the poet's advice and is an imperative. Since the battle will be lost with much loss of blood:

Keep your head down and stay indoors -
we've lost this war before it has begun.

Hardi uses personal pronouns (*we* and *us* as opposed to *they* and *them*) to highlight the opposition between the community and the attacking army units.

The tone of the poem begins in fearful anticipation and moves to futility: the young Kurdish fighters have only *rusty guns* to defend their community with. Hardi communicates a strong and despairing sense of what will happen when the enemy arrives – and it is all the more shocking because of its inevitability and unavoidability. However, in addition to these tones, I do not think it fanciful to sense a mood of community solidarity in the poem too: the village may be threatened but there is a strong sense of togetherness in their shared suffering. Hardi's tone remains one of calm and defiant stoicism throughout, mixed with righteous anger.

Why?

In this moving poem Choman Hardi:

- portrays a beleaguered village nervously awaiting an attack by superior forces.
- conveys a strong sense of community solidarity in the face of violent and unprovoked aggression.
- displays an acute awareness of the effects of the attack on the inhabitants.
- adopts a tone of fear and resignation tempered by determination and stoicism – we get the sense that the community will survive, despite many of the villagers being killed.

Endings

This may seem like an obvious point, one hardly worth drawing attention to, but you have seen from the poems discussed above that the endings of poem are absolutely vital and crucial to their overall effect. In 'The Sick Rose' the final word – *destroy* – carries threat and menace. You will find in many of the poems in the Anthology the ending – the final stanza, the final line, the final sentence, even sometimes the final word – changes what has gone before and forces us to see things differently. So be aware of this as you read and as you revise. When you are writing about poems, the way they end and the emotional conclusion they achieve is a simple way to compare and contrast them. It may not be easy to express what it is exactly that they do achieve, but make sure you write something about the endings, because the endings are often the key to the whole poem. Remember – a poem (like a song) is an emotional journey and the destination, the ending, is part of the overall message, probably its most important part.

'A Poison Tree' – William Blake

Author & Context

William Blake (1757 – 1827) is now seen as the foremost artist and poet of his time, but his work was largely unknown during his lifetime. He was a painter as well as a poet and you can see some of his paintings in art galleries like Tate Britain in London or the Fitzwilliam Museum in Cambridge. 'London' comes from a collection called *Songs of Innocence and of Experience*, which appeared together for the first time in 1794. *The Songs of Innocence* (which originally appeared on their own in 1789) are positive in tone and celebrate unspoilt nature, childhood and love. *The Songs of Experience* (from which 'A Poison Tree' comes) depict a corrupt society in which the prevailing mood is one of despair, children are exploited and love is corrupted.

Blake was writing at a time when Britain was the wealthiest country in the world because of its global empire and because of the Industrial Revolution which produced goods which were exported all over the world. But not everyone shared in this enormous wealth; the gap between rich and poor was huge, with the poor suffering really terrible living and working conditions. *The Songs of Innocence and of Experience* first 'appeared' (this term will be explained below) in 1794. The date of publication is crucial: Blake is partly seeing London in this way because of events in France. In 1789 the French Revolution began, changing French society forever and ushering in a new age of freedom, equality and brotherhood. Many English people saw what was happening in France and thought it was good to have a society based on greater equality; they looked critically at British society and saw appalling inequalities and injustices. For example, you may be aware that this was the period in British history that some people campaigned against slavery in the British Empire: what is less well-known is that forms of slavery existed in London. There are recorded cases of parents selling their sons to master chimneysweeps in London. The life of a chimney sweep was likely to be short: they were sent up the chimneys of large houses to clean them. Some suffocated; others were trapped in the confined space and died; sometimes their masters would light fires below them to encourage them to work faster – they sometimes were burnt alive. For those who survived, their health was affected: they suffered from terrible lung complaints as a result of breathing in coal dust and, because of poor hygiene, might also succumb to testicular cancer brought on by the accumulated layers of biting coal dust. Apart from being in favour of the slogans of the French Revolution, evidence from his other writings would suggest that Blake was in favour of openness and honesty. Think back to 'The Sick Rose' discussed in the introduction: the rose harbours a "dark, secret love" and is annihilated by the "invisible worm".

Blake had produced *Songs of Innocence* on its own in 1789, although we can tell from his surviving notebooks that he always intended to write *Songs of Experience*. I have used the term 'appeared' because they were not published in a conventional sense. Blake produced each copy of *Songs of Innocence and of Experience* at home by hand and copies were then given to friends and acquaintances. Part of this was Blake's own choice, but we can easily see that his views about Britain and its government would have been highly controversial, so open publication of them may have led to charges of sedition or treason. The British government at the time were terrified of a revolution here, like the one in France, and were doing everything they could to silence people like Blake who were critical of the society in which they lived.

Blake earned his living as an engraver. Before photographs and modern ways of reproducing images, engravings were the cheapest and easiest way of illustrating a book. Blake produced illustrations for other people's books throughout his life – that was how he earned a living. To create an engraving, the engraver has to carve, with a specialist knife, lines on a metal plate; when the plate is then covered in ink and pressed on paper the lines appear on the paper.

On page 40, you can see (in black and white) Blake's illustration for 'a Poison Tree'. Many of the illustrations to Songs of Experience are quite dark in tone and atmosphere, but the overall impression of 'A Poison Tree' is one of light, which, as we will see below, may be connected with the poem's themes and message

Blake used the same technique for reproducing his own poems. After coating the metal plate with ink and producing the outline, Blake coloured each page of each copy of *Songs of Innocence and of Experience* by hand with water colour paint. It is estimated that only 25 copies were produced in his lifetime. If you go to the British Museum you can see one copy: it is tiny and exquisitely detailed and, of course, very personal, because Blake coloured it by hand himself. In addition, to produce his poems in this way was time-consuming and arduous, since in order for the words to appear the right way round when the page was printed, they had to be written in mirror hand-writing on the plate – a painstaking process that must have taken hours and shows not only Blake's artistry but also his devotion to hard work.

wrath – anger

foe – enemy

wiles – tricks and deceit

stole – crept

When the night had veiled the pole – when clouds had darkened the night sky so that even the Pole Star could not be seen.

Who? The speaker tells a simple story about how his untold anger for an enemy grew and grew until it killed the enemy.

When? No specific time: the poem appeared first in 1794.

Where? No specific location but the metaphor of the tree symbolizing his anger suggests a garden setting.

What? Blake is angry with a friend but tells him so and the anger passes away. He is also angry with an enemy but says nothing. His anger for his enemy grows and grows; Blake uses the metaphor of a plant to describe his growing anger – an anger which he feeds with his hypocritical reactions to his enemy. The tree becomes an apple tree and one night his enemy steals into his garden and plucks the apple. This action ends in his death.

When you first read Blake's 'A Poison Tree' you may be astonished at its simplicity, but, as we will see, Blake uses a simple form and simple language to make a complex statement about how we deal with anger and its effects.

In the first stanza, the situation is clear: the speaker was angry with a friend with whom he was open about his anger and their disagreement and his anger subsided. He was also angry with his foe, but said nothing, kept his anger hidden and, once it is hidden, it grows. The two couplets are perfectly balanced in terms of rhyme, the number of syllables, the repetition of words and even the exact placing of the caesura in lines 2 and 4.

In the next two stanzas, Blake uses anaphora: seven of the eight lines begin with *and,* as he excitedly describes what happens to his wrath. In the second stanza he introduces a metaphor: his wrath is a plant and he *water'd it in fears* and *sunned it with smiles/And soft deceitful wiles.* The speaker's disagreement with his friend makes him fearful, makes him cry with rage and frustration, but he still appears outwardly friendly, showering his enemy with *smiles,* showing him to be hypocritical and deceitful.

The third stanza fleshes out the metaphor of the plant which now *grew day and night.* The anaphora of *and* does create a sense of excited enjoyment – this is a process which not only involves hypocrisy but the enjoyment of that hypocrisy. The tree grows an apple and Blake tells us:

And my foe beheld it shine,

And he knew that it was mine.

In the final stanza, the foe creeps into the garden, steals the apple and dies – a sacrifice to secrecy, hypocrisy and deceit. What is most disturbing is that the speaker is glad. To be glad at someone's misfortune – let alone death – shows an evil and unhealthy attitude.

The poem consists of four quatrains with each quatrain made up of two rhyming couplets. Basically the poem is written in trochaic tetrameters. 'Tetrameter' simply means there are four stressed syllables in each line; trochaic means that the pattern of stresses is a stressed syllable followed by an unstressed syllable; however, Blake uses variations on this basic pattern to reflect what is happening in the poem. Normally we would expect a tetrameter line to have eight syllables – four stressed and four unstressed – but Blake only writes three lines with eight syllables: lines two, four and the last line of the poem. So what? I hear you say. Well, it means that each line, which is short, seems a little incomplete and it is masterful of Blake to utilise these short lines in most of the poem – he is describing an incomplete process - the slow and steady growth of his anger (the tree), so he is describing an ongoing, incomplete process – just as the lines themselves are incomplete by being one syllable too short. To further vary the metrical pattern lines two, four and the last line are perfect iambic tetrameters. Why? Because they describe a situation or action which is complete or has been resolved.

The original draft of 'A Poison Tree' in Blake's 'Notebooks' had the title 'Christian Forbearance' suggesting that tolerance for something or someone you disagree with is a good thing, but might also be covering up anger or disapproval. Blake felt that traditional Christians who were taught to be pious could easily be hypocritical, masking their true feelings beneath superficial friendliness. In the poem, the speaker's hypocrisy leads to the death of his enemy. The title 'Christian Forbearance' is clearly intended to be sarcastic.

The main theme of 'A Poison Tree' is not anger in itself (we are given no reason for the speaker's anger) but how the suppression of anger is harmful and dangerous. Repressing anger rather than being honest and open about it transforms anger into a seed, which will grow into a tree. The growth of the seed is made possible by the energetic anger of the speaker into a destructive force. Blake pursues the metaphor of a growing plant when he writes *and I water'd it in fears/Night and morning with my tears* his foe makes him fearful and cry tears of rage. The speaker also says *I sunned it with smiles*: on the surface he is polite to his foe and smiles at him. The metaphor works because plants need water and sunlight to thrive. But this deceit and hypocrisy must take its toll on the speaker.

The tree in 'A Poison Tree' is meant to remind the reader of the Tree of the Knowledge of Good and Evil in the Biblical story of the Fall of Man. God forbids Adam or Eve to eat the fruit of that tree, but Eve disobeys and Adam and Eve are expelled from the Garden of Eden. This event is known as the Fall of Man and is responsible (in Christian belief) for bringing death and sin into the world. As far as the poem is concerned, the speaker takes the wrathful, vengeful attitude to his enemy – acting in a way that is reminiscent of the God of the Old Testament. [Blake was a devout Christian but his views were rather unorthodox: basically, he thought the God of the Old Testament was evil, but the God of the New Testament – Jesus – was the true God.] In this poem, we can say that Blake gives his speaker the attitudes and outlook of the wrathful God of the Old Testament. It may be significant here that the foe is lying on the floor with his arms outstretched – very like the crucified Christ.

If the poem has a message it is not only the importance of expressing your anger and not stifling it. It also demonstrates that the suppression of feelings of anger will lead to a corruption of those feelings, through secrecy and deceit, to a corruption of innocence.

Conflict

The obvious source of conflict in the poem is that between the speaker and his enemy, but there are other more subtle conflicts at work in the poem. Firstly, there is the speaker's own division of the people he knows into friends and foes – we have no knowledge about how he makes this distinction, but it is built into characterising the people we know as friend or foes. More egregiously there is conflict within the speaker himself, due to his lack of honesty and his superficial friendliness towards his foe – the *smiles* that he gives the foe and which, in the poem, allow the tree to grow. The effort to be nice to someone he loathes causes the speaker to cry tears which also help the tree and the resentment grow. Therefore, the theft of the apple not only kills the foe, the process leading up to it – the strain and hypocrisy of pretending to be nice to your enemy – takes a psychological toll on the speaker, so that he has lost all human empathy and is glad to see his foe dead alongside the tree.

A Romantic Poem

Blake's work is very different from the poetry of the other Romantic poets. However, the simplicity of language marks this out as a

Romantic poem: Wordsworth had experimented with simple language in *Lyrical Ballads*, first published in 1798, and in that collection Samuel Taylor Coleridge's famous poem 'The Rime of the Ancient Mariner' had made use of Christian symbolism as Blake does here. More generally, Blake's call for openness and his criticism of authoritarian power and hypocrisy places this poem firmly within the Romantic poetic spectrum.

Why?

In this short but complex poem, Blake:

- attacks hypocrisy.

- attacks secrecy.

- shows how the suppression of anger can have worse consequences than its expression.

- praises openness and honesty in personal relationships.

- by implication attacks the Old Testament God for his harsh, forbidding attitude to humanity.

'Envy' – Mary Lamb

Author & Context

Mary Lamb was born in 1764 and died in 1847. She and her brother Charles Lamb wrote collections of stories and poems together, often for children, including *Tales from Shakespeare* and *Poems for Children*.

Mary suffered from mental illness - perhaps what we would now call bipolar disorder. She was cared for by her family, but was institutionalised at different points during her life. She killed her own mother during a period of mental instability in 1796.

Many of her poems for children resemble nursery rhymes. The history of nursery rhymes goes back hundreds of years but in the 19th century, rhymes for children were very popular. These included books written specifically for children. Many nursery rhymes contain messages and lessons hidden in simple stories and straightforward rhymes.

Envy – ill-will and hostility at the looks, attributes and accomplishments of another.

mignionet – a sweet scented type of grass.

Who? The poet writes as herself to, we assume, an audience of children.

When? No specific location.

Where? No specific time.

What? The poet warns against feelings of envy.

Commentary

Envy is one of the Seven Deadly Sins and in this short, straightforward poem for children Lamb seeks to dissuade her readers from feelings of envy.

Lamb uses a rose tree as a metaphor for envy. In the first verse she observes that *the rose-tree is not made to bear/ The violet blue, nor lily fair.* And if the rose tree were to express envy over what it cannot do then

... and if this tree were discontent.
Or wished to change its natural bent,
*   It all in vain would fret.*

The second stanza picks up on this idea of fretting and being envious, and argues that the rose is unaware of its own beauties and qualities:

... you would suppose
It ne'er had seen its own red rose
Nor after gentle shower
Had ever smelled its rose's scent,
Or it could ne'er be discontent
With its own pretty flower.

Awareness of one's own qualities will prevent feelings of envy.

In the third stanza Lamb makes explicit (for her audience of children) and asserts that *All envious persons* are like the *blind and senseless* rose tree.

The moral of the poem is made clear in the final three lines – and that is that we can all find something to value about ourselves which is unique to ourselves:

With care and culture all may find
Some pretty flower in their own mind,
Some talent that is rare.

The poem consists of three verses and rhymes AACCDD in the first verse; the second and third verses rhyme AACDDC. This is a didactic and moralistic poem, and Lamb suits her vocabulary and the simplicity of her rhyme scheme to her audience of children. The imagery of flowers is straightforward enough to be understood by children.

Conflict

Envy is a very negative emotion which can cause conflict. If you are envious of someone else, this can cause feelings of hostility and resentment. Furthermore, feelings of envy cause internal conflict in the envious person because it can damage their sense of self-worth and their self-esteem. Therefore, envy is responsible for external and internal conflict.

Why?

In 'Envy' Mary Lamb:

- writes a simple poem with simple imagery and vocabulary perfectly suited to her audience of children.

- encourages people with low self-esteem to take pride in their achievements.

- uses the simple imagery of flowers to make her moral point.

- writes a didactic, moralistic poem.

- reinforces Christian values (Envy is one of the Seven Deadly Sins).

'Boat Stealing' (from 1799 *Prelude*) – William Wordsworth

Author & Context

William Wordsworth was born in 1770 in Cockermouth on the edge of the English Lake District. He had a life-long fascination with nature and it is from the natural world that he took much of his inspiration. He died in 1850, having been made Poet Laureate in 1843. Wordsworth began to write *The Prelude* in 1798 and kept working on it and revising it until his death. It was not published until 1850, three months after his death. He published many poems during his own lifetime, but many readers feel that *The Prelude* is his finest work.

This extract is from *The Prelude*, a long autobiographical poem first finished in 1805. It is subtitled *The Growth of the Poet's Mind* – and Wordsworth tells the story of his life but with the intention of showing his psychological development and also how he came to be a poet. Central to his development, he claims, was the influence of nature: Wordsworth grew up in the English Lake District – a national park and an area of outstanding natural beauty even today. It is not just that Wordsworth liked the beauty of nature – we perhaps all do that because we associate it with peace, away from the hustle and bustle of urban or suburban life; he also believed that nature had a moral influence on him and had made him a better human being. He is at pains throughout *The Prelude* to try and prove this connection – that his experiences in the natural world made him a better person and a poet. You may elsewhere read references to Wordsworth's pantheism. Pantheists worship nature and feel that if there is a God then that God exists in every living thing, every part of the natural world: God is a spirit of the universe which exists in a rock or a daffodil as much as it does in a human being.

her – Nature.

elfin pinnace – a pinnace is a small boat; elfin means small and charming.

covert – secret.

bark – boat.

Who? The poet narrates in the past tense an incident from his childhood.

When? 1805. Wordsworth was a child in the late 18th century but is recollecting this experience as an adult.

Where? On a lake in the English Lake District, generally thought to be Ullswater.

What? Wordsworth steals a boat and goes for a row on the lake. He explores the ramifications of this incident on his conscience.

Commentary

This extract is written in blank verse. It narrates an incident. This extract comes from Book II of *The Prelude* which is entitled *Childhood and School-Time*. The opening sentence clearly shows the influence of Nature on the young Wordsworth:

One summer evening (led by her) I found

A little boat tied to a willow tree.

However, this quotation comes from the 1850 version of The Prelude. I have used it here for two reasons: firstly, to show that poetry is not fixed – poets change their minds; secondly, to show the importance of nature to Wordsworth. We know that *her* refers to nature from the preceding lines. The poet proceeds to unchain the boat and take it for an illicit row on the lake. In effect, Wordsworth is stealing the boat: he describes it as *an act of stealth* (he doesn't want to get caught) and uses an oxymoron – *troubled pleasure* – to show us that he has mixed feelings about what he is doing: he knows it is wrong. Lines 8–11 use a variety of sound effects and very positive vocabulary to present the initial experience of this escapade. He says the boat left behind her

still on either side,

Small circles glittering idly in the moon,

Until they melted all into one track

Of sparkling light.

Listen to those lines: Wordsworth uses no figurative language, but there is a preponderance of *s*, *l* and *m* sounds which give a gentle, restful feeling which reinforces the meanings of the words. The lines are given more aural coherence by assonance: *side/idly/light* and by consonance – *track/sparkling*. Wordsworth has decided to row across the lake and has picked out a craggy ridge as his landmark towards which he is heading.

This positive tone and atmosphere continues up to line 20. The boat is an *elfin pinnace* – playful, mischievous (like an elf) – and the boat moves through the water *like a swan* – a beautiful, majestic bird.

And then the whole tone changes. By a trick of perspective, as Wordsworth rows across the lake, a huge peak comes into view. When you row, you face the direction you started from and the further Wordsworth rows from the shore of the lake, the mountains behind his starting point start to appear. Look at how the poet describes it and his response to it:

a huge peak, black and huge,

As if with voluntary power instinct,

Upreared its head. I struck and struck again,

And growing still in stature the grim shape

Towered up between me and the stars, and still,

For so it seemed, with purpose of its own

And measured motion like a living thing,

Strode after me.

Like nature, like the boat, the peak is personified and takes on a life of its own, but note also the way a sense of panic in the poet is created by simple repetition of *huge* and *struck*; these lines are full of sibilance too, which creates a sinister, hissing sound. Wordsworth's reaction is one of guilt and shame:

With trembling oars I turned,

And through the silent water stole my way.

He puts the boat back where he found it and then finds he is haunted by this experience for many days afterwards. He does not fully understand what has happened to him:

my brain

Worked with a dim and undetermined sense

Of unknown modes of being.

He is also depressed by the experience:

In my thoughts

There was darkness, call it solitude

Or blank desertion.

He cannot take his customary pleasure in nature – *No familiar shapes remained* – and his every waking thought and even his sleep is disturbed by:

> *... huge and mighty forms that do not live*

Like living men, moved slowly through the mind

By day, and were a trouble to my dreams.

How are we to interpret this poem? If some of the language towards the end of the extract seems a little vague, it is because Wordsworth himself – as a small boy – is struggling to make sense of what happened to him.

What is certain is that this experience is a formative one and leads to an epiphany: the poet is made to feel guilty for taking the boat and in that sense it is an important part of Wordsworth's intention – to show that we can learn morality from nature – not just from books or other people. And so nature is presented as beautiful and inspiring but also frightening if you do something wrong or immoral. The huge and mighty forms that haunt the young boy's mind in the days that follow the incident seem to suggest that there is a divinity in nature, that the natural world (as Wordsworth sees it) is an expression of the existence of God and one which punishes us when we commit immoral acts – like stealing someone else's boat.

We can also see this extract as charting the passage from innocence to experience, from childhood to adulthood. In the first part of the extract Wordsworth is totally in control – of the boat, the situation and his emotions. What he is doing may be wrong but it is clearly enjoyable for a brief period: this can be seen as showing how attractive it is to sin – we are tempted to do wrong because some sins are very attractive and pleasurable. But the sudden appearance of the mountain changes everything and shows the young poet that he is not in control: there is a higher power that watches over us. In simpler terms, we might say that the mountain symbolises his guilty conscience.

Conflict

This extract is remarkable for the power that Nature has over the young Wordsworth. Nature's influence makes him feel guilt for his casual theft of the boat and exerts a moral influence on him lasting for a long time after the incident. The long poem – *The Prelude* (from which this is an extract) – is full of examples of nature's influence on Wordsworth's spiritual and moral development, demonstrating Wordsworth's Pantheism. The conflict centres around the theft of the boat, and it really involves the internal conflict and guilt that Wordsworth feels and which is heightened by Nature and the looming crag that seems to rise up and overpower him. Wordsworth's personification, his animation of Nature, greatly aids the impression on the reader.

A Romantic Poem?

This extract is typically Romantic as is the whole of *The Prelude*. The very act of writing a long autobiographical poem about himself suggests that Wordsworth considers himself an exceptional individual with important truths to convey through his poetry. The supreme importance given to nature – in this passage and elsewhere in *The Prelude* – also marks it out as typically romantic, as does Wordsworth's pantheistic notion that Nature is a living force that can inculcate morality.

Why?

This very famous extract:

- shows nature as a moral and spiritual guide.

- explores the psychology of a young boy and his intense feelings of guilt.

- the importance it attaches to Nature make it a typically Romantic poem.

- explores the attractiveness of wrong-doing, but also the effects of a guilty conscience.

- demonstrates a deep love of and respect for nature.

- focuses very closely on the individual and his relationship with nature.

- depicts vividly the beautiful exuberance of rowing across the lake in the moonlight;

- focuses very closely on the individual and his relationship with nature;

- demonstrates the inner conflict Wordsworth feels after doing something wrong – stealing a shepherd's boat for a joy-ride on the lake;

- demonstrates the beauty of nature.

'The Destruction of Sennacherib' – Lord Byron

Author & Context

Byron was the ideal of the Romantic poet, gaining notoriety for his scandalous private life and being described by one contemporary as 'mad, bad and dangerous to know'.

George Gordon Noel, sixth Baron Byron, was born on 22 January 1788 in London. His father died when he was three, with the result that he inherited his title from his great uncle in 1798.

Byron spent his early years in Aberdeen and was educated at Harrow School and Cambridge University. In 1809, he left for a two-year tour of a number of Mediterranean countries. He returned to England in 1811, and in 1812 the first two cantos of 'Childe Harold's Pilgrimage' were published. Byron became famous overnight and very wealthy from the high sales his poetry achieved. He achieved what we would now term 'celebrity status', but public opinion was soon to turn against him.

In 1814, Byron's half-sister Augusta gave birth to a daughter, almost certainly Byron's. The following year Byron married Annabella Milbanke, with whom he had a daughter, his only legitimate child. The couple separated in 1816.

Facing mounting pressure as a result of his failed marriage, scandalous affairs and huge debts, Byron left England in April 1816 and never returned. He spent the summer of 1816 at Lake Geneva with Percy Bysshe Shelley, his wife Mary and Mary's half-sister Claire Clairmont, with whom Byron had a daughter.

Byron travelled on to Italy, where he was to live for more than six years. In 1819, while staying in Venice, he began an affair with Teresa Guiccioli, the wife of an Italian nobleman. It was in this period that Byron wrote some of his most famous works, including 'Don Juan' (1819-1824).

In July 1823, Byron left Italy to join the Greek insurgents who were fighting a war of independence against the Ottoman Empire. On 19 April 1824, he died from fever at Missolonghi, in modern day Greece. His death was mourned throughout Britain. His body was brought back to England and buried at his ancestral home in Nottinghamshire.

Much of the Old Testament in the Christian Bible, from which Byron took the bare bones of this story, concerns the efforts of the Israelites or Jews to withstand enemies who wanted to conquer their land or take them into captivity as slaves. This story is no exception. In the Bible, the Second Book of Kings, Chapter 18, verse 13 the story begins:

Now in the fourteenth year of King Hezekiah did Sennacherib King of Assyria came up against the fenced cites of Judah and took them.

There then follows an extremely long account of negotiations and diplomacy – which Byron judiciously omits – and the story comes to an end in the Second Book of Kings, Chapter 19, verse 35:

And it came to pass that night that the angel of the Lord went out and smote in the camp of the Assyrians an hundred four score and five thousand: and when they arose early in the morning, behold, they were all dead.

It is this miraculous divine intervention that forms the inspiration for Byron's poem.

If you want to read this poem in context *Hebrew Melodies* is available in a cheap paperback version.

Sennacherib – the main god worshipped by the Assyrians and the name of one of their emperors whose reign was from 705 BCE to 681 BCE.

Assyrian - Assyria was a major Mesopotamian East Semitic kingdom, and empire, of the Ancient Near East, existing as an independent state for a period of approximately six centuries from c. 1250 BCE to 612 BCE, spanning the Early Bronze Age through to the late Iron Age. For a further thirteen centuries, from the end of the 7th century BC to the mid-7th century AD, it survived as a geo-political entity. It covered most of what is now Syria and Iraq.

fold – a fenced enclosure usually holding sheep.

cohorts – troops of soldiers.

host – army.

on the morrow – on the next day.

strown – disordered

waxed – became.

steed – horse.

mail – chain mail armour.

Ashur – another god worshipped by the Assyrians and also the name of one of their major cities and one-time capital.

Baal – another God worshipped by the Assyrians.

The Gentile – 'Gentile' is a Jewish term used to cover all those who are non-Jews, in this case the defeated Assyrian army.

unsmote – 'unhit' by human swords, arrows, lances and other weapons.

Who? Sennacherib besieged Jerusalem in 701 BCE. The speaker narrates a story which is well-documented in the Old Testament. He speaks directly to the modern reader and assumes an air of authority.

When? Byron published the poem in 1815, as part of a collection called *Hebrew Melodies*. The collection was published twice – as a book of poems and also as a book of songs with the music written by the Jewish composer Isaac Nathan.

Where? In Judea, the historic land of the Jews, now roughly covered by the state of Israel and Palestine.

What? The mighty Assyrian army attacks Jerusalem but is destroyed by divine intervention – the angel of the Lord.

Commentary

The Assyrian Empire was very militaristic and aggressive in expanding their empire. Byron's opening simile *like the wolf on the fold* – suggests an evil, animalistic aggressor quickly bearing down on an innocent and defenceless innocent. Their troops present an impressive sight: *gleaming in purple and gold*. Then, in the third line of the first stanza, Byron uses sibilance to give the line cohesion, but the fact that *their spears were like stars on the sea* suggests the sheer size of the army.

In the second stanza, it contains an abrupt contrast between the two couplets: in the first couplet the Assyrian army looks grand and magnificent: *Like the leaves of the forest is green,* but in the second couplet and on the morning of the next day the army has been transformed – *Like the leaves of the forest when Autumn has blown.*

In the third stanza, Byron reveals what has happened to the once-mighty army. The Angel of Death has *breathed in the face of the foe as he passed* and the Assyrians are all dead:

... the eyes of the sleepers waxed deadly and chill,

And the hearts but once heaved, and for ever grew still.

The next two stanzas emphasise the complete destruction of the Assyrian army. In the fourth stanza, the horses that carried the Assyrians into battle are foaming at the mouth and as *cold as the spray of the rock-beating surf.* In the fifth stanza, the Assyrian soldiers lie dead with *the dew on his brow, and the rust on his mail.* The mighty army is now all dead and their encampment is destroyed and Byron emphasises this by describing their camp:

... the tents were all silent, the banners alone,

The lances unlifted, the trumpet unblown.

Despite their military superiority and their wonderful appearance (as suggested in the first stanza) the Assyrian army has been destroyed by the Angel of Death sent by God.

The final stanza describes the reaction in Ashur, the Assyria capital is shown: the widows of the dead soldiers are *loud in their wail* and the statues of Baal are destroyed in their temples. The Assyrians worshipped several Gods and worshipped idols of them – unlike the Jews who worshipped a single God and who were banned from worshipping statues or idols of him in the Ten Commandments. The materialistic Assyrians have been defeated by the true God – they *Have melted like snow in the glance of the Lord!*

'The Destruction of Sennacherib' is a very regular poem, consisting of six stanzas each with four lines. Each line has twelve syllables and

Byron chooses to write in anapaestic tetrameters. Tetrameter means that there are four stressed syllables in each line. Anapaestic refers to the arrangement of stresses in each line of the poem. An anapaest consists of two unstressed syllables followed by a stressed syllable:

And his **cohorts** *were* **gleaming** *in* **purple** *and* **gold**

Here I have emboldened the stressed syllables. But why? What is the effect of this metrical patterning? Firstly, when read aloud the poem generates a quick speed which is very appropriate for a narrative poem – the rhythm pushes us on to the next stage of the story. Secondly and more importantly, the speed mimics the speed of the Assyrian army as it approaches Jerusalem – it may even be said to mimic the speed and rhythm of the horses of its army approaching. Thirdly, and perhaps most important of all, the rhythm and its speed suggest the speed of the Assyrian defeat and devastation at the hands of the Angel of Death. In general, the rhythm helps give us an aural sense of the urgency of the situation facing Jerusalem and the speed at which the events unfold.

The rhyme scheme is AABB: the first two lines in each stanza rhyme with each other as do the third and fourth lines. This apposition of lines is powerful and suggests the opposition between the invading Assyrian army and Jerusalem and its defenders. Byron also uses anaphora at the start of many of his lines – *like, the* and *and* – *then* and *and* - are especially appropriate in a narrative poem describing a quick series of events.

Conflict

The conflict in this poem is straightforward between Judea and Jerusalem and the powerful conquering army of the Assyrians. The tone of the poem is one of triumph and celebration at the deliverance from military conquest of Jerusalem and the Jewish people.

A Romantic Poem?

Before he published *Hebrew Melodies* Byron was best known for long narrative poems, so to publish a collection of short lyric poems was not typical of him. Byron was also known as a radical free thinker, so it is ironic that he should choose a story from the Old Testament. Indeed, this poem is the most famous poem on a Biblical subject to be produced by any English Romantic poet. Coleridge and Wordsworth were avowedly Christian but neither produced a poem like 'The Destruction of Sennacherib'. Blake, as we have seen, was a Christian but held esoteric and unconventional ideas about God, especially the God of the Old Testament.

And so the poem is not typical of Byron and is an oddity when judged against the work of the other English Romantic poets.

Some readers argue that the arrogance and might of the Assyrian army is analogous to the power and threat to peace posed by the French emperor Napoleon. However, Byron was a political radical and the government of Britain at the time was increasingly tyrannical and oppressive, so if the poem has any contemporary significance, it is probably a reminder to British conservative politicians that their days are numbered.

Why?

In this fast and dramatic narrative poem, Byron:

- makes brilliant use of metre and rhythm to capture both the quick approach of the Assyrian army and its quick and ruthless destruction by the Angel of Death.

- takes a fairly obscure story from the Bible and writes an exciting, thrilling poem whose speed gives the whole poem narrative verve and purpose.

- uses similes well to describe the invading army.

- at the end paints a vivid picture through words of the desolation of the Assyrian camp.

'There's a Certain Slant of Light' – Emily Dickinson

Author & Context

Emily Dickinson was born into a financially sound family where she had a privileged and comfortable life. She closed herself up from publicity and led an isolated life. Emily Dickinson attended both Amherst Academy and Mount Holyoke Female Seminary. However, she wrote pretty well and her early writings were mostly letters of which very few got published during her lifetime. Her poetry was known for its unconventional style. She used slant rhymes, unconventional punctuation, capitalization, short lines and some lacked titles as well. Her poems mostly centred on her struggles with her faith, morality, her father and the challenges she had to face as a woman. She has emerged as a major American woman poet. The two major themes of her poem are death and immortality. The first and complete collection of her poetry was published in 1955, *The Poems of Emily Dickinson* by scholar Thomas H. Johnson.

Heft – weight

the Seal Despair – a Biblical reference: Revelations 6.5.

Structure and syntax

The extensive use of dashes and unconventional capitalization in Dickinson's manuscripts, and the idiosyncratic vocabulary and imagery, combine to create a body of work that is "far more various in its styles and forms than is commonly supposed". Dickinson avoids pentameter, opting more generally for trimeter, tetrameter and, less often, dimeter. Sometimes her use of these meters is regular, but oftentimes it is irregular. The regular form that she most often employs is the ballad stanza, a traditional form that is divided into quatrains, using tetrameter for the first and third lines and trimeter for the second and fourth, while rhyming the second and fourth lines (ABCB). Though Dickinson often uses perfect rhymes for lines two and four, she also makes frequent use of slant rhyme. In some of her poems, she varies the meter from the traditional ballad stanza by using trimeter for lines one, two and four, while only using tetrameter for line three.

Since many of her poems were written in traditional ballad stanzas with ABCB rhyme schemes, some of these poems can be sung to fit the melodies of popular folk songs and hymns that also use the common meter, employing alternating lines of iambic tetrameter and iambic trimeter. Familiar examples of such songs are "O Little Town of Bethlehem" and "Amazing Grace'".

Morbidity

Dickinson's poems reflect her "early and lifelong fascination" with illness, dying and death Perhaps surprisingly for a New England spinster, her poems allude to death by many methods: "crucifixion, drowning, hanging, suffocation, freezing, premature burial, shooting, stabbing and guillotinage" She reserved her sharpest insights into the "death blow aimed by God" and the "funeral in the brain", often reinforced by images of thirst and starvation. Dickinson scholar Vivian Pollak considers these references an autobiographical reflection of Dickinson's "thirsting-starving persona", an outward expression of her needy self-image as small, thin and frail. Dickinson's most psychologically complex poems explore the theme that the loss of hunger for life causes the death of self and place this at "the interface of murder and suicide".

Commentary

This poem is about *a certain Slant of light* that the speaker notices on winter afternoons. However, this light is malign – it is like *the Heft/ Of Cathedral Tunes* and it oppresses. The rest of the poem explores what sort of oppression this is.

The slant of light gives *Heavenly Hurt* to the onlooker: it gives no physical hurt (*We can find no scar*), but causes psychological or spiritual change – *internal difference*. This internal difference cannot be taught by a third party - it must be experienced. Although the insight brings *Despair*, Dickinson describes it as *An imperial affliction/ Sent us of the air*. There is a sense in which *imperial affliction* is an oxymoron or at the very least an unusual collocation, *imperial* suggesting something grand and important, while *affliction* suggesting something unpleasant. When the insight comes it is powerful enough to make the landscape listen and shadows to hold their breath, and when it goes

... tis like the Distance

On the look of Death –

The poem consists of four quatrains and Dickinson uses a rhyme scheme – ABAB – but with some half-rhymes. Perhaps the half-rhymes are there to suggest the unsettling experience she undergoes.

When the *imperial affliction* comes *the Landscape listens* and *Shadows – hold their breath*. When it goes

...'tis like the Distance

On the look of Death –

Death may be a long way away, but the distance – which may be short or long – is evoked by a certain slant of light on winter afternoons.

Conflict

The main conflict in the poem is between the fear of death and the process of death and the prospect of everlasting life in Heaven. The slant of light in the context of a late afternoon in winter acts as a premonition of death – something that will come but is not predictable and that will lead to Heaven, but is frightening in itself. Despite the fact that the slant of light oppresses and leads to melancholy thoughts, the tone of the poem remains calm and controlled.

Why?

In this poem Emily Dickinson:

- uses her succinct, elliptical style to reflect on very profound issues.

- as so often in her poetry, she takes one small thing – here a slant of light – as the starting point of her poem.

- maintains a calm tone despite the gravity of the subject matter.

'The Man He Killed' – Thomas Hardy

Author & Context

Thomas Hardy (1840 – 1928) is best known as a novelist. He wrote 15 novels, most of which are set largely in Dorset and the surrounding counties, and which deal with the ordinary lives of ordinary people in stories in which they struggle to find happiness and love – often battling against fate or their own circumstances. His final two novels *Tess of the D'Urbervilles* (1891) and *Jude the Obscure* (1895) both portray sex outside marriage in a sympathetic way and there was such a hysterical public outcry about the novels that Hardy stopped writing fiction and devoted the rest of his life to poetry. Although some of his poetry is intensely personal, this poem is also typical of his work in that it gives a voice to an ordinary man. Although Hardy trained as an architect, he came from a fairly poor family and, in both his novels and his fiction, he never forgets his roots – often making the rural poor central characters in his novels or giving them a voice in his poetry, as he does here.

Who? The speaker of the poem is an ordinary, working class man who joined the army. The poem is a dramatic monologue.

When? Hardy wrote the poem in 1902 when Britain was fighting the Boers in South Africa in the Second Boer War. The Boers were settlers of Dutch descent who did not want to be subsumed within the British Empire. British public opinion was divided on the issue of the Boer

War – Hardy saw it as the British, motivated by South Africa's gold and diamond mines, meddling in the affairs of independent settlers who were simply trying to defend their homes and did not want to be part of the British Empire. Hardy opposed the war.

Where? There is no indication of where the speaker is (although given the poem itself and its contents, one can imagine the poem being part of an anecdotal pub conversation). The action of the poem takes place on an unnamed battlefield.

What? The speaker of the poem tells an anecdote about a man he killed during a war. The poem is a dramatic monologue, addressed seemingly to an acquaintance of the speaker and attempts to explain why the speaker killed a man in warfare.

inn – pub, public house.

nipperkin – a measure of beer roughly equivalent to a third of a pint and most common in the West Country.

foe – enemy.

'list – enlist in the army.

Off-hand – casually, without serious conviction.

sold his traps – the speaker assumes the man joined the army because he had sold his traps – presumably traps to catch rabbits and other game.

quaint – strange.

half a crown – an old unit of currency.

Commentary

In the first stanza, the speaker admits that the man he killed and he would probably have enjoyed a drink together:

Had he and I but met

By some old ancient inn.

However, as they met in war-time as infantry soldiers *staring face to face*, they shot at each other and the speaker *killed him in his place.*

In the third stanza, the speaker tries to offer an explanation of why he shot the man:

I shot him dead because —

Because he was my foe.

The repetition of *because* suggests that the speaker is uncertain that this is a good enough reason, a point underlined by his statement in the third and fourth lines:

…my foe of course he was;

That's clear enough.

But the next word is *although* as the speaker and former soldier realises there is some fault in his logic; Hardy then uses enjambment from the third stanza to the fourth as the man's train of thought continues and he realises (despite the man being called his *foe*) that the man he killed probably had a lot in common with him: that the man enlisted *Off-hand like – just as I* or perhaps he was simply out of work.

The repetition of *because* also suggests hesitation and a lack of certainty, while the word *foe* (repeated twice) suggests that it is not the man's word: he has been told by propaganda that the men they are fighting are his *foe*. The phrase *my foe* is repeated too, which suggests perhaps that he is trying to convince himself of the justice of what he did or that he has heard the word used by a senior officer – both possibilities might be true. Hardy foregrounds the word *foe* not just through repetition but also through the internal rhyme with *so* in line three of the third stanza. The final line of the stanza is *No other reason why* and, although Hardy's speaker is too naïve to follow this thought to its logical conclusion, those simple words – *No other reason why* – explode all the myths about why men fight for their country: honour, glory, a sense of duty, patriotism, loyalty to one's King or Queen, loyalty to one's country or to one's flag. All these are exposed as lies by the simple words of Hardy's ex-soldier. Hardy's speaker cannot articulate these arguments but he does observe in the final stanza *How curious and quaint war is,* because it pits men who might have much in common – who, indeed, might have shared a beer together - but calls them the *foe* who must be killed. This is a profoundly anti-war poem.

The other reason war is shown to be less than heroic are the reasons the speaker tells us for joining the army: being out of work or having sold one's traps – *No other reason why* – which completely undercuts all the patriotic reasons for which men supposedly joined.

Hardy chooses to use the ballad stanza in the poem: a simple quatrain with a rhyme scheme of ABAB in each stanza. This ancient, egalitarian form is appropriate to his speaker. Hardy's language is also appropriately chatty and colloquial: there are no metaphors or similes – Hardy is imitating the voice of a working class soldier.

The structure of the poem is significant. The first stanza opens with a positive tone; the picture of two men perhaps enjoying a beer together at a traditional English inn is a positive one. The second stanza shatters this by revealing that the speaker killed the man. The third stanza attempts to provide a justification for the killing his *foe*, while the fourth speculates that they had *perhaps* some shared reasons for enlisting in the army – such as being out of work. The final stanza ends the poem, but all Hardy's working class soldier can conclude is that war is *quaint and curious*. Hardy's use of a relatively inarticulate common soldier is important: the reader can see that war (put in the soldier's terms) is absurd and futile but these are words his speaker would never use. Therefore, the structure of the poem (we might say) moves from casual and light, to casual and dark – a human being has died. It remains casual because of the speaker's colloquial language and his simple explanation for what he did.

Neither soldier is named nor are the armies they are fighting for identified. It is clear that the speaker is intended to be English, but the poem arguably has a universal feel to it – that it could apply to any war in any century. The dashes in the fourth stanza are important too: they are examples of ellipsis: the words they separate are shortened forms and help to give an impression of a real speaker. However, coming after *perhaps* in the first line of the stanza it is also as though the speaker is hesitantly realising that he and the man he killed had a lot in common. The poem uses several parallel structures and repetition – *I shot at him as he at me*, *face to face* and *off-hand like just as I*. The most important parallel structure – that the two men are essentially very similar is implied throughout the poem.

Hardy's use of a working class soldier is absolutely vital to the effect of this poem. Both the speaker and the man he killed have been following orders given to them by their officers from higher classes. If a state of war did not exist, then they would have enjoyed a beer together. And where does the word *foe* come from: it would appear to be a word the soldier has heard from a superior officer or perhaps read in a newspaper, which are so keen to whip up jingoistic sentiment in a time of war.

Conflict

The war and the man the speaker kills are the obvious conflict in the poem; however, there is another conflict – within the speaker himself. Although he attempts to justify the killing – he was his *foe* and they were *ranged as infantry/And staring face to face* – his efforts to do this are rather naïve. The man he killed is still someone with whom he could have enjoyed a few beers. His conclusion – *How quaint and curious war is* – is naïve because, as we are well aware, wars do not simply happen, politicians decide that they should happen and send men to their deaths. Therefore, because of the speaker's lack of understanding, there is likely to be a conflict between his stated view of war and the readers'.

Why?

This short but powerful poem by Hardy:

- uses a working class soldier to expose the futility and absurdity of war.

- shows that the demonisation of the enemy as the *foe* is an important device to justify murder.

- demonstrates that the working classes of different countries have more in common than their rulers or those (the government) who choose to go to war.

- demonstrates the dreadful randomness of warfare: the two men were "staring face to face" and one was lucky enough to live.

- uses colloquial language throughout the poem to give a realistic sense of the speaker's voice.

'Anthem for Doomed Youth' – Wilfred Owen

Author & Context

Wilfred Owen (1893 – 1918) is widely regarded as the leading British poet of the First World War. He died in action on November 4th 1918 – just seven days before the war finally came to an end. Owen was an officer and was awarded the Military Cross for leadership and bravery in October 1918. The shock of what he saw in the front-line moved him to produce a great many poems in a very short time – most of which were not published until after his death. He seems to have been particularly keen to ensure that the British public was told the horrific truth about the war. He developed his own use of half-rhyme which was to influence other poets for the whole of the 20th century. Owen famously wrote that his subject was not war, but the pity of war – a feeling that is especially apparent in this poem. "Above all I am not concerned with Poetry. My subject is War, and the pity of War. The Poetry is in the pity."

It is over a hundred years since the First World War began, and, because of the many commemorations, many readers will have a visual sense of what that war was like. In fact, it was a world war with fighting taking place on almost every continent, but the abiding memory of the war – a memory based on photos, documentaries and even poems like this one, is of the trench warfare on the Western Front in Belgium and France. There are clear reasons for this. The war waged in the trenches resulted in battles with enormous loss of life with very little ground gained: on the first day of the Battle of the Somme the British army suffered 70,000 casualties, 20,000 of whom were killed. I think the other reason the Western Front holds such an important place in our image of the First World War is the trenches themselves and trench life: hundreds of thousands of soldiers living very close to each other in holes in the ground and suffering terrible, barbaric conditions, plagued by rats, lice and the cold. So the futility and loss of life in the battles, as well as the appalling conditions make the war in the trenches especially memorable.

passing-bells – the single tolling bell rung at funerals.

orisons – an archaic word for prayers.

shires – British Army infantry regiments were based on the counties and shires, so if you came from Lincolnshire you fought in the Lincolnshire regiment.

pallor – extreme paleness, here out of grief.

pall – the cloth used to cover the coffin; in a formal military ceremony this would be the Union Jack.

a drawing down of blinds – it was tradition, when there was a death in the family to draw all the curtains.

Who? Owen writes as himself to a general audience.

When? The First World War, probably 1917.

Where? On the Western Front.

What? Owen compares and contrasts the funerals the dead soldiers would receive if they were buried at home in England with the hasty, makeshift funerals they receive on the battlefields in France.

Commentary

'Anthem for Doomed Youth' is probably the best poem wrote about the war, and it is possibly the best poem to be written about the war. It is a Petrarchan sonnet – which for me adds to its emotional impact. considered by many to be the highest form of poetry (because of the difficulty of composing one): that such a beautiful form should be used to write about the tragedy of the war increases its impact.

We are fortunate to have a copy of Owen's first draft of the poem and I want to look at three changes he made which improved the poem. As you can see the original title was 'Anthem for Dead Youth'. What does Owen gain from changing it to 'Doomed'? Well, he includes those already dead as well as the those who are doomed to die in the future. He also introduces assonance in the 'ooo' sound of both words which foreshadows the sound of the *monstrous guns*. The first line in the draft is *What passing bells for those who die so fast?* Owen changed this by using a simile comparing the men to cattle.

What does he gain from this? Well, he preserves the sense of speed – cattle are killed very quickly at the abattoir – but the simile introduces two new ideas: that the cattle are killed in large numbers and that they have no choice in the matter – ideas which relate directly to the men on the Western Front. The start of the last line originally *And every dusk*, but Owen changed it to *And each slow dusk*. This has to be said more slowly and mirrors the slowness of the dusk he is describing.

The poem is based on an extended contrast with a conventional funeral, so Owen gives aspects of a funeral their sad, heart-rending parallel in the terrible conditions of the battlefield. Because of the war, there was not time to bury bodies properly – indeed, many were buried in mass graves and some bodies were simply never found, leading the soldier to have no known grave. The Thiepval Monument lists the 72,000 British soldiers who died on the Somme but who have no known grave.

The doomed soldiers have no passing bells, only the *monstrous anger of the guns*: the guns are transformed into monsters and there is a hint of onomatopoeia in *monstrous anger*. The third line uses alliteration and onomatopoeia to give a sense of the sounds of battle – and asserts that this is what the soldiers will have instead of their final prayers to God. The *stuttering rifles' rapid rattle* imitates the sound of gunfire in battle.

Line 5 insists there be *No mockeries for them; no prayers or bells*. Owen seems to be implying that to have a proper, funeral service would be a mockery, given the way these men have fought and died, in huge numbers and horrific conditions. They will have no choirs to sing at their funerals only the

The shrill, demented choirs of wailing shells;

And bugles calling from them from sad shires.

Note the onomatopoeia in *shrill* and *wailing* – this poem is rich in literary techniques. They will be missed in their native counties where bugles will call - in vain - for them.

There is a turn or volta in line 9 at the start of the third quatrain as Owen turns his attention to the friends and loved ones the soldiers will leave behind. There will be no candles held in the hands of boys for these dead soldiers

> *...but in their eyes*

Shall shine the holy glimmers of goodbyes.

Their comrades' eyes will be filled with tears which will shine. Their coffins will have no pall which will be replaced by *The pallor of girls' brows* – pale from the shock and sadness at the news of their husbands' or boyfriends' deaths.

The final couplet is especially moving:

Their flowers the tenderness of patient minds,

And each slow dusk a drawing down of blinds.

They will have no flowers at their funerals. They will be replaced by *tenderness* – the emotion which is the exact opposite of their experiences as soldiers and as corpses; it is unclear who the *patient minds* belong to – perhaps their surviving companions, perhaps their loved ones at home. In the final line the slowness created by *each slow dusk* emphasizes the action it describes, while in the final phrase the repeated 'd' sounds give an aural harmony to the end of the poem.

Conflict

The conflict that was the First World War forms the background to the poem and Owen conveys superbly the sounds and horrors of that war. However, the main conflict in the poem is the disparity between the funerals the dead soldiers would expect to get at home in normal circumstances and the rushed, undignified funerals they receive on the battlefield. That is where the pity of the poem lies.

Why?

In 'Anthem for Doomed Youth' Owen has

- written an elegy for a generation and evoked pity for them all.

- written a perfect Petrarchan sonnet.

- written a poem rich in assonance, alliteration and onomatopoeia which adds greatly to its emotional impact.

- used a comparison throughout the poem – the burial the soldiers do get on the battlefield compared with the funerals they would expect at home.

- ended the poem on a note of tenderness, pity and compassion.

'Vergissmeinnicht' – Keith Douglas

Author & Context

Keith Castellain Douglas (24 January 1920 – 9 June 1944) was an English poet noted for his war poetry during the Second World War and his wry memoir of the Western Desert campaign, '*Alamein to Zem Zem*'. He was killed in action during the invasion of Normandy. This poem was written in Tunisia in May to June 1943 when Douglas was fighting the German Afrika Korps in the northern Sahara. Douglas was a tank commander.

Douglas described his poetic style as "extrospective", that is, he focused on external impressions rather than inner emotions. The result is a poetry which, according to his detractors, can be callous in the midst of war's atrocities. For others, Douglas's work is powerful and unsettling because its exact descriptions eschew egotism and shift the burden of emotion from the poet to the reader. His best poetry is generally considered to rank alongside the 20th century's finest soldier-poetry.

Vergissmeinnicht – forget me not.

Steffi – the name of the German soldier's girlfriend.

abased – humbled, degraded.

swart – black.

Who? Douglas writes as himself as he re-visits the site of the three-week-old battle, and reflects on the decaying corpse of a dead German soldier.

When? The summer of 1943.

Where? Tunisia, North Africa.

What? Douglas focuses on the body of a dead German soldier, and a photo of his girlfriend which is lying strewn about, and contrasts the feelings of himself and the other British soldiers with the likely reaction of his girlfriend.

Commentary

This poem is highly organized to the eye but not to the ear. It consists of six quatrains. Douglas uses half-rhyme, slant rhyme and full rhyme – but not in a consistent way in each stanza. This irregularity, it could be argued, reflects the chaos of war, but more importantly the poet's own very mixed emotions as he describes what he sees: Douglas's feelings are a mixture of triumphalism – he killed a soldier who was trying to kill him – but also compassion and pity for the dead man and for his girlfriend.

In the first stanza Douglas and his men revisit the site of a skirmish with the enemy three weeks beforehand. The battle must have been traumatic since Douglas calls it a *nightmare ground* and they come across the corpse of a dead German *soldier sprawling in the sun* – the sibilance on 's' adding a sinister feeling to the line. Sprawling suggests an air of laziness and satisfied content, but this soldier is dead and decaying.

The dead soldier is overshadowed by *the frowning barrel of his gun.* Here the personification of the gun adds to its menace, and the opening sentence of the second stanza contains no finite verb, suggesting that the threat still exists – from other Germans. Douglas remembers the day of the encounter with this enemy force and this soldier in particular

As we came on

That day, he hit my tank with one

like the entry of a demon.

The simile adds to the sense of threat and danger that Douglas felt at the time of the battle. Along with *nightmare ground* from the first verse Douglas conveys how terrifying the experience was and how it continues to effect him.

The third stanza starts with an abrupt *Look* as Douglas spots in the gunpit the photo of the German doldier's girlfriend who has signed the photo *Steffi. Vergissminicht* – Steffi. Forget me not.

Stanza four returns to the attitudes of the British soldiers. Douglas writes:

We see him almost with content,

abased, and seeming to have paid

and mocked at by his own equipment

that's hard and good when he's decayed.

A key phrase here is *almost with content*: they are almost happy to see the dead German decaying and note the irony that he is decaying while his equipment is hard and good. War is a brutal thing and both sides were trying to kill each other. It could be argued that one of Douglas's strengths as a war poet is his unflinching honesty. But the key word is *almost*: the last two stanzas demonstrate compassion for the soldier's girlfriend and for the soldier himself.

Despite the sense of contentment as soldiers in stanza four, Douglas has sufficient imagination to know that the soldier's girlfriend

… would weep to see today

how on his skin the swart flies move;

the dust upon the paper eye

and the burst stomach like a cave.

These gruesome details make clear the horrific reality of war and the vulnerability of the human body in death. The irony, noted earlier, that his equipment is solid and hard underlines the essential frailty of the human body.

The poem's final stanza is justly famous. In it Douglas observes that we often in life have more than one role – here the German soldier is both Steffi's lover and a killer for the German army. The British soldiers can be happy that the killer is dead and abased, but feel sorrow that the human being, Steffi's lover, is dead;

For here the lover and killer are mingled

who had one body and one heart.

And death who had the soldier singled

has done the lover mortal hurt.

The clear implication is that all soldiers in the war are potential killers but lovers too, and while the soldiers must kill or be killed, it is a tragedy that the lovers have to die too. The title of the poem can be seen to stand for all dead soldiers in the war.

Conflict

The setting of the poem is a major conflict: the Second World War. However, the central conflict in the poem is within the poet: he feels a sense of triumph at his enemy's death (at which he is *almost content*), but is still capable of feeling compassion at the death of another human being. The poem cannot resolve this conflict.

Why?

In this poem Douglas:

- conveys the sheer randomness of war – he could have been killed himself in the initial encounter.

- through the decaying body of the German soldier conveys the horror and brutality of war.

- through his use of the photograph of the dead soldier's girlfriend, conveys a sense of the man's individuality.

- uses a dispassionate tone until the very end of the poem where a tone of moral ambiguity creeps into the poem: Douglas killed an enemy soldier (as a soldier that is his job).

- the poem and the title is a fitting epitaph for all soldiers who died in the war.

- writes one of the best poems to emerge from the Second World War.

'What Were They Like?' – Denise Levertov

Author & Context

Denise Levertov (24 October 1923 – 20 December 1997) was a British-born American poet. During the course of a prolific career, Denise Levertov created a highly-regarded body of poetry that reflects her beliefs as an artist and a humanist. Her work embraces a wide variety of genres and themes, including nature lyrics, love poems, protest poetry, and poetry inspired by her faith in God. Levertov was born and grew up in Ilford, Essex. Her mother, Beatrice Adelaide (née Spooner-Jones) Levertoff, came from a small mining village in North Wales. Her father, Paul Levertoff, had been a teacher at Leipzig University and as a Russian Hassidic Jew was held under house arrest during the First World War as an 'enemy alien' by virtue of his ethnicity. He emigrated to the UK and became an Anglican priest after converting to Christianity. In the mistaken belief that he would want to preach in a Jewish neighbourhood, he was housed in Ilford, within reach of a parish in Shoreditch, in East London. His daughter wrote, "My father's Hasidic ancestry, his being steeped in Jewish and Christian scholarship and mysticism, his fervour and eloquence as a preacher, were factors built into my cells". Levertov, who was educated at home, showed an enthusiasm for writing from an early age and studied ballet, art, piano and French as well as standard subjects. She wrote about the strangeness she felt growing up part Jewish, German, Welsh and English, but not fully belonging to any of these identities. She notes that it leant her a sense of being special rather than excluded: "[I knew] before I was ten that I was an artist-person and I had a destiny". She noted: "Humanitarian politics came early into my life: seeing my father on a soapbox protesting Mussolini's invasion of Abyssinia; my father and sister both on soap-boxes protesting Britain's lack of support for Spain; my mother canvasing long before those events for the League of Nations Union; and all three of them working on behalf of the German and Austrian refugees from 1933 onwards... I used to sell the *Daily*

Worker house-to-house in the working class streets of Ilford Lane". The *Daily Worker* was a Communist newspaper and in the Spanish Civil War a socialist government fought a war against fascist rebels - who won and who imposed a brutal fascist dictatorship on Spain.

When she was five years old, she declared she would be a writer. At the age of 12, she sent some of her poems to T. S. Eliot, who replied with a two-page letter of encouragement. In 1940, when she was 17, Levertov published her first poem. During the Blitz, Levertov served in London as a civilian nurse. Her first book, *The Double Image*, was published six years later. In 1947, she met and married American writer Mitchell Goodman and moved with him to the United States the following year. Although Levertov and Goodman would eventually divorce in 1975, they did have one son, Nikolai, together and lived mainly in New York City, summering in Maine. In 1955, she became a naturalised American citizen and is considered an American poet. She achieved fame through a series of books which dealt with the Vietnam War.

Vietnam had been a French colony until 1954. When the French withdrew a civil war broke out between Communist North Vietnam and capitalist South Vietnam. North Vietnam's aim was to unite the country, South Vietnam's to preserve its independence. However, this took place during the Cold War and America intervened (initially with military advisers) in order to help South Vietnam and to stop the spread of Communism. However, the South Vietnamese were clearly losing the war. So in 1964 the USA began to bomb North Vietnam and in 1965 it sent 200, 000 combat troops to Vietnam. The heavy bombing of North Vietnam continued: in May 1964 the American general, Curtis Le May, said in a quotation that became notorious: *Tell the Vietnamese they've got to draw in their horns or we're going to bomb them back to the Stone Age.*

As the 1960s wore on, the Americans committed more and more troops to Vietnam until there were half a million there by 1968.

However, although the USA was the world's military superpower and possessed military technology that was far superior to the North Vietnamese army, it was clear that North Vietnam were winning the war by using hit-and-run guerrilla tactics and avoiding large-scale open battles with the American army.

Back home in the USA, the war became increasingly unpopular and a growing anti-war movement quickly grew and huge public protests were held. Marshall McLuhan, a cultural commentator, said in 1975:

TV brought the brutality of war into the comfort of the living room. Vietnam was lost in the living rooms of America – not on the battlefields of Vietnam.

From 1970, America began to withdraw its troops but continued to bomb North Vietnam with its aircraft. By 1973, all American ground troops had been withdrawn, leaving only advisers. By 1975, the North Vietnamese Army seized the capital of South Vietnam, Saigon, and the war was over and the country was unified. America's military might have been humiliated.

This poem (published in 1971) is part of domestic American protest against the Vietnam War.

jade – is a semi-precious rock, usually green in colour, which is used to make ornaments and jewellery.

paddies – flooded fields in Asia used to grow rice.

epic poem – a long narrative poem which tells of brave and heroic deeds.

Who? There are two speakers: the first asks questions which form the first stanza; the second answers each question in turn and in detail. We cannot tell who the speakers are but it is clear that the first speaker holds some sort of authority or importance because the second speaker addresses him as *Sir*.

When? In an imagined future in which America has won the war and completely obliterated Vietnam, its people and culture.

Where? There is no specific location.

What? The questions are asked to ascertain the truth about the Vietnamese way of life and culture.

The first question is:

Did the people of Vietnam

use lanterns of stone?

To which the answer is;

Sir, their light hearts turned to stone.

it is not remembered whether in gardens

stone gardens illumined pleasant ways.

Their light hearts turning to stone is an effect of the war. The passive voice of *it is not remembered* is chilling here as is the implication the pleasant ways no longer exist because they have been destroyed.

The second question is:

Did they hold ceremonies

to reverence the opening of buds?

The answer is:

Perhaps they gathered once to delight in blossoms,

but after their children were killed

there were no more buds.

A response that is full of anguished empathy for the child victims of the war.

The questioner asks: *Were they inclined to quiet laughter?* which elicits the response *Sir, laughter is bitter to the burned mouth* – a line which manages to suggest both the physical suffering of the Vietnamese (*burned mouth*) and their psychological suffering – they have forgotten how to laugh.

The next question – *Did they use bone and ivory / jade and silver for ornament?* – elicits a longer answer:

> *Ornament is for joy.*
>
> *All the bones were charred,*
>
> *it is not remembered. Remember,*
>
> *Most were peasants; their life*
>
> *was in rice and bamboo.*
>
> *When peaceful clouds were reflected in the paddies*
>
> *and the water buffalo stepped surely along terraces,*
>
> *maybe fathers told their sons old tales.*

I have quoted this answer at length because it gives us a more complete picture of how Levertov presents the Vietnamese people in the poem: they are presented by the poet as simple, innocent, gentle people living a humble and simple existence; however close that may be to the truth is irrelevant: in the poem and in the poem's context Levertov's presentation of their way of life like this is a direct and peaceful contrast to the destructive military might of the American Army with its ability to bomb the Vietnamese into surrender. They have no epic poem, although Levertov speculates that *fathers told their sons tales* – the past tense is significant since they no longer tell their sons tales because they no longer exist as a people.

The final question is: *Did they distinguish between speech and singing?* The respondent says that their speech was *like a song* and their singing *resembled moths in moonlight* – a gentle, peaceful image. But the truth is that no one knows because *it is silent now*. In Levertov's imagined future, Vietnamese culture and its people have been wiped out.

The poem is written in free verse which is appropriate as the respondent struggles to give coherent answers to the questions asked.

This poem became rapidly famous when it was published in 1971. Some readers felt she was being slightly patronising to the Vietnamese – who had a fully developed cultural life and were not all simple peasants; however, that is to miss the point of the poem, I think. The poem is for an American audience and it serves as a piece of anti-war propaganda and, in contrast to the brutality of American mass bombing of North Vietnamese cities, Levertov is quite consciously trying to create sympathy and empathy for the Vietnamese.

Conflict

This poem deals with the aftermath of a conflict and, within the poem itself, there is little conflict – but it only came to be written because of the Vietnam War. We might sense a minor conflict in the poem between the dryly academic and dispassionate questions of the opening stanza, and the answering voice which is keen to provoke sympathy and empathy for the Vietnamese people. There are also oblique references to the effects of the conflict between the USA and North Vietnam: *their children were killed*; *the burned mouth*; *All the bones were charred* and *When bombs smashed those/Mirrors there was only time to scream*. And thus the second voice gives us details of the conflict designed to shock the reader.

Why?

This poem by Denise Levertov:

- is set in an imaginary future (North Vietnam actually won the war and ejected the Americans).
- is a poem which protests about American tactics and involvement in Vietnam.
- arouses sympathy for the Vietnamese people.
- warns against the possible genocide of the Vietnamese people and uses chilling images to suggest that eventual fate.

'Lament' – Gillian Clarke

Author & Context

Gillian Clarke who was born in 1937 in Cardiff is one of the leading poets of our time and is very much associated with Wales, where she has lived for most of her life. She and her husband live on a smallholding and keep sheep. You can find a lot of very useful material for students on her website, including comments on most of her poems. Her writing is deeply rooted in everyday experience – sometimes personal experience – but also touches on wider, deeper themes. Her poetry is widely studied in schools and she gives regular poetry readings and lectures about poetry.

Gillian Clarke is one of the central figures in contemporary Welsh poetry, the third to take up the post of National Poet of Wales. Her own poems have achieved widespread critical and popular acclaim (her *Selected Poems* has gone through seven printings and her work is studied by GCSE and A Level students throughout Britain) but she has also made her cultural mark through her inspirational role as a teacher, as editor of the *Anglo-Welsh Review* from 1975-1984, and as founder and President of Ty Newydd, the writers' centre in North Wales. Born in Cardiff and currently running an organic small-holding in Ceredigion, the Welsh landscape is a shaping force in her work, together with recurrent themes of war, womanhood and the passage of time. Her last three books have all been Poetry Book Society Recommendations.

Clarke's world is full of the here-and-now - the scratch of stubble at a young girl's ankles ('Letter from a Far Country'), the slipperiness of a newborn lamb ('A Difficult Birth'), emotion experienced as bodily sensation, "the tight red rope of love" ('Catrin'). However, immediate as the poems are, they are also haunted by many different kinds of past which re-surface in the present like the drowned girl given the kiss of life in 'Cold Knap Lake'.

This poem is about the First Gulf War, also known as the 1991 Gulf War. Gillian Clarke has said:

"'Lament' is an elegy, an expression of grief. It can be a sad, military tune played on a bugle. The poem uses the title as the start of a list of lamented people, events, creatures and other things hurt in the war, so after the word 'lament', every verse, and 11 lines, begin with 'for'. The poem is about the Gulf War, which happened in 1991 when Iraq invaded Kuwait, and the United States, with Britain's help, bombed Iraq. This war has never really stopped. As we begin a new school year, it still threatens the world. War can't be waged without grave damage to every aspect of life. All the details in the poem came from reports in the media. There were newspaper photographs of cormorants covered with oil - 'in his funeral silk'. 'The veil of iridescence on the sand' and 'the shadow on the sea' show the spreading stain of oil from bombed oil wells. The burning oil seemed to put the sun out, and poisoned the land and the sea. The 'boy fusilier who joined for the company,' and 'the farmer's sons, in it for the music', came from hearing radio interviews with their mothers. The creatures were listed by Friends of the Earth as being at risk of destruction by oil pollution, and 'the soldier in his uniform of fire' was a horrific photograph of a soldier burnt when his tank was bombed. The ashes of language are the death of truth during war."

The First Gulf War

The Gulf War (2 August 1990 – 28 February 1991), codenamed Operation Desert Shield (2 August 1990 – 17 January 1991), for operations leading to the buildup of troops and defense of Saudi Arabia and Operation Desert Storm (17 January 1991 – 28 February 1991) in its combat phase, was a war waged by coalition forces from 34 nations led by the United States against Iraq in response to Iraq's invasion and annexation of Kuwait. In purely military terms the war was a success the Iraqis being forced to give up Kuwait. In human and environmental terms, however, the war was a disaster.

Gulf War oil spill

The Gulf War oil spill was one of the largest oil spills in history, resulting from the Gulf War in 1991.The apparent strategic goal was to foil a potential landing by US Marines. It also made commandeering oil reserves very difficult for US forces. The immediate reports from Baghdad said that American air strikes had caused a discharge of oil from two tankers. Coalition forces determined the main source of oil to be the Sea Island terminal in Kuwait. On January 26, three US F-117 fighter-bombers destroyed pipelines to prevent further spillage into the Persian Gulf. Several other sources of oil were found to be active: tankers and a damaged Kuwaiti oil refinery near Mina Al Ahmadi, tankers near Bubiyan Island, and Iraq's Mina Al Bakr terminal.

Environmental impact

Early estimates on the volume spilled ranged around 11,000,000 US barrels (1,300,000 m^3). These numbers were however significantly adjusted downward by later, more detailed studies, both by government (4,000,000 US barrels (480,000 m^3) to 6,000,000 US barrels (720,000 m^3) and private (2,000,000 US barrels (240,000 m^3) to 4,000,000 US barrels (480,000 m^3)) researchers. The slick reached a maximum size of 101 miles (160 km) by 42 miles (68 km) and was 5 inches (13 cm) thick in some areas. Despite the uncertainty surrounding the size of the spill, figures place it several times the size (by volume) of the Exxon Valdez oil spill.

The New York Times reported that a 1993 study sponsored by UNESCO, Bahrain, Iran, Iraq, Kuwait, Oman, Qatar, Saudi Arabia, the United Arab Emirates and the United States found the spill did "little long-term damage": About half the oil evaporated, 1,000,000 US barrels (120,000 m^3) were recovered and 2,000,000 US barrels (240,000 m^3) to 3,000,000 US barrels (360,000 m^3) washed ashore, mainly in Saudi Arabia.

More recent scientific studies have tended to disagree with this assessment. Marshlands and mud tidal flats continued to contain large quantities of oil, over nine years later, and full recovery is likely to take decades.

Dr. Jacqueline Michel, US geochemist (2010 interview – transcript of radio broadcast):

The long term effects were very significant. There was no shoreline cleanup, essentially, over the 800 kilometers that the oil – - in Saudi Arabia. And so when we went back in to do quantitative survey in 2002 and 2003, there was a million cubic meters of oil sediment remained then 12 years after the spill.... [T]he oil penetrated much more deeply into the intertidal sediment than normal because those sediments there have a lot of crab burrows, and the oil penetrated deep, sometimes 30, 40 centimeters, you know a couple of feet, into the mud of these tidal flats. There's no way to get it out now. So it has had long term impact.

Dr. Hans-Jörg Barth, German geographer (2001 research report):

The study demonstrated that, in contrary to previously published reports e.g. already 1993 by UNEP, several coastal areas even in 2001 still show significant oil impact and in some places no recovery at all. The salt marshes which occur at almost 50% of the coastline show the heaviest impact compared to the other ecosystem types after 10 years. Completely recovered are the rocky shores and mangroves. Sand beaches are on the best way to complete recovery. The main reason for the delayed recovery of the salt marshes is the absence of physical energy (wave action) and the mostly anaerobic milieu of the oiled substrates. The latter is mostly caused by cyanobacteria which forms impermeable mats. In other cases, tar crusts are responsible. The availability of oxygen is the most important criteria for oil degradation. Where oil degrades it was obvious that benthic intertidal fauna such as crabs re-colonize the destroyed habitats long before the halophytes. The most important paths of regeneration are the tidal channels and the adjacent areas. Full recovery of the salt marshes will certainly need some centuries.

Kuwaiti oil fires

Oil well fires rage outside Kuwait City in 1991.

The Kuwaiti oil fires were caused by the Iraqi military setting fire to 700 oil wells as part of a scorched earth policy while retreating from Kuwait in 1991 after conquering the country but being driven out by Coalition forces. The fires started in January and February 1991 and the last one was extinguished by November 1991.

The resulting fires burned out of control because of the dangers of sending in firefighting crews. Land mines had been placed in areas around the oil wells, and a military cleaning of the areas was necessary before the fires could be put out. Somewhere around 6 million barrels (950,000 m³) of oil were lost each day. Eventually, privately contracted crews extinguished the fires, at a total cost of US$1.5 billion to Kuwait. By that time, however, the fires had burned for approximately ten months, causing widespread pollution.

Lament – to utter grief, to mourn, an elegy or dirge.
iridescence – a play of rainbow colours like petrol in some water puddles.
dugong – a herbivorous marine mammal

Who? The poet speaks as herself.

When? In 1991 during the First Gulf War.

Where? The Persian Gulf, Kuwait and Iraq.

What? Clarke writes a lament for all the creatures harmed by the First Gulf War, with the emphasis on the environmental impact.

Commentary

The examiners want you to respond to the poem, but I have devoted a lot of space to the context, so you are in full possession of the facts and you realize that what the poem describes really happened.

'Lament' is a simple poem in its structure. It consists of seven stanzas each of three lines each. The lines are roughly equal in length, but there is no set rhyme scheme or rhythmical pattern, reflecting perhaps the chaos and confusion of war. A lament is a song of grief and Clarke grieves that the war ever took place. In doing so she displays empathy and sympathy for all life caught up in the war – humans, birds, marine life and the environment in general.

The first stanza focuses on the green turtle, searching for her *breeding ground*. Her *pulsing burden* are the eggs she is attempting to lay, but because of the war and the damage to the environment she is forced to lay them in a *nest of sickness*. *Nest of sickness* is a particularly arresting phrase with oxymoronic qualities, since we associate nests with places of safety and security.

The second stanza deals with the oil spillages caused by the war by concentrating on a cormorant, a sea bird, *in his funeral silk* – his plumage is covered in oil. The *shadow on the sea* is the dark area caused by the oil spill.

Clarke widens her perspective in the third stanza. She writes of the *ocean's lap with its mortal stain* – the stain of the oil spill- in the first line. In the second line she recognizes the human suffering that the war causes:

For Ahmed at the closed border.
For the soldier with his uniform of fire.

Uniform of fire is especially effective in conveying the horror of war.

The fourth stanza continues with the human participants of the tragedy that is war, including soldiers who joined the army never expecting to fight, such *the boy fusilier who joined for the company* and *the farmer's sons in it for the music*. As has been already said Clarke shows sympathy and empathy for all life caught up in the destructiveness of war.

In the fifth stanza Clarke simply lists marine life affected by the war: *the hook-beaked turtles, the dugong and the dolphin*. The last line is especially poignant:

the whale struck dumb by the missile's thunder.

Whales sing to each other and many people find recordings of whale songs strangely beautiful and peaceful, so for the whale to be struck dumb is a real tragedy.

Clarke's poem is actually very simple in form. It consists of seven verses and is written in free verse, although the line lengths are broadly similar. Each stanza starts with the word *For*, because what follows in each stanza is the subject of Clarke's lament. Each verse is designed to elicit sympathy and grief for the victims of the war – human, animal and environmental.

The first stanza focuses on the green turtle searching for somewhere to lay her eggs, but finding all the beaches polluted by oil spills – *their nest of sickness.*

The second stanza focuses on an oil-covered cormorant (his ironic and oxymoronic *funeral silk*), the petrol stains on the sand and the oil-spill on the sea – *the shadow on the sea.*

The third stanza introduces a slight variation as every line starts with *For.*

For the ocean's lap with its mortal stain –

all the environmental damage caused by oil spills and mis-directed missiles.

For Ahmed at the closed border.

Many Iraqis were taken prisoner: as the notes in the context suggest the war was easily won and the Iraqi army suffered disproportionate losses and most poignantly...

For the soldier with his uniform of fire.

The fourth stanza focuses closely on human victims of the war, especially those who joined the Iraqi army not expecting to die in a war, such as *the boy fusilier who joined for the company.*

The fifth stanza returns to the animal kingdom lamenting the hook-beaked turtles, the dugong and the dolphin and *the whale struck dumb by the missile's thunder:* all of which were affected by the enormous environmental damage the war caused.

The fifth stanza focuses on birds - their fruitless *long migrations and the slow dying* that being covered in oil condemns them to. The *veiled sun* is a reference to the Kuwaiti oil fires which obscured the sun. *The stink of anger* is a particularly striking phrase, referring as it does to the burning oil wells and the stink of dead bodies – both human and animal.

The final stanza acts as a summary and conclusion:

For the burnt earth and the sun put out,
the scalded ocean and the blazing well.

And the last line

For vengeance, and the ashes of language.

Vengeance is against Iraq for its illegal invasion of Kuwait. *The ashes of language* phrase is, I think, a reference to euphemistic military jargon which was used during the war to conceal a grim and sad reality. For example, 'friendly fire' became commonplace during the war – it means being attacked by your own side; similarly, 'collateral damage' was used to describe civilian targets which were accidentally bombed or suffered damage when a legitimate military target was bombed. These are the *ashes of language* because they obscure the truth and make the events sound almost good. For example, to be hit by friendly fire sounds quite good – it's friendly, after all – but it is no consolation if you die from friendly fire. Even the notion of 'winning' a war that does so much damage to life and to the planet becomes, in the context of the poem, a painful distortion of language.

Conflict

The man-made conflict of war kills and maims men and women fighting in it, but it also causes a massive impact on the environment which Clarke is keen to highlight. All the creatures mentioned in the poem have been effected by the war – a man-made conflict which causes damage and long-term harm to the eco-system.

Why?

- Clarke's poem is successful, I feel, because of its simplicity and its memorable phrases. Its simplicity lies in its form – it is essentially a list, but it gains its power from being based closely on true, genuine events.

- Clarke' shows empathy for all living things caught up in the war – from humans to turtles.

- Clarke's poem raises awareness about the environmental damage that human wars cause – a fact that often gets forgotten or ignored in the media's rush to report on the progress of the war itself.

A sea bird trapped in oil.

'Punishment' – Seamus Heaney

Author & Context

Seamus Heaney was born on 13 April 1939 and died on 30 August 2013. Heaney was an Irish poet, widely recognized as one of the best poets writing in English in the late 20th and early 21st centuries. He was awarded the Nobel Prize for Literature in 1995. He was born and brought up in Northern Ireland, but lived in the Republic of Ireland from 1973. Heaney considers himself an Irish poet and has objected to being included in collections of 'British' poets. Northern Ireland has had a violent and troubled history, but Heaney's poems (even those which do address political concerns) are always deeply personal and rooted in everyday events and circumstances.

Robert Lowell described him as "the most important Irish poet since Yeats", and many others, including the academic John Sutherland, have echoed the sentiment that he was "the greatest poet of our age". Robert Pinsky has stated that "with his wonderful gift of eye and ear Heaney has the gift of the story-teller." Upon his death in 2013, *The Independent* described him as "probably the best-known poet in the world."

His body is buried at the Cemetery of St. Mary's Church, Bellaghy, County Londonderry. The headstone bears the epitaph "WALK ON AIR AGAINST YOUR BETTER JUDGEMENT".

First published in *North* (1975), 'Punishment' takes its inspiration from a corpse discovered, fully preserved in the peat bogs of Jutland, western Denmark. Heaney read *The Bog People* (1969), an account by P. V. Glob, the archaeologist who carried out the excavations and who attempted to explain the significance of the ritual murders the perfectly-preserved corpses bore witness to. 'Punishment' focuses on the body of a young woman who was executed and, halfway through the poem, Heaney speculates that she may have been punished for adultery.

halter – a rope around her neck for controlling her.

amber – solid resin from trees used to make jewellery and ornaments.

rigging – her rib-cage – like the ropes on a sailing ship.

weighing – a large stone held her body down and branches were strewn on top.

barked sapling – a young tree stripped of all its bark.

oak-bone – when the body was excavated the archaeologists found it difficult to distinguish wood from preserved flesh.

brain-firkin – her skull; a small casket holding her brain.

tar-black – the corpse has been stained black by the peat bog.

scapegoat – a reference to the Old Testament practice of the ritual driving away of a selected goat to take away the sins of the tribe.

stones – In Biblical times adulterers were stoned to death. In the New Testament, Jesus, on being asked whether an adulteress should be punished in the traditional way, answered. "He that is without sin among you, let him cast the first stone."

voyeur – someone who takes pleasure from observation rather than direct participation, especially of sexual or sex-related acts.

brains… combs – the brains were extracted for detailed examination.

webbing – netting.

numbered – in an archaeological excavation every item is numbered so that, in this case, the bodies, can be reassembled.

cauled – covered or painted in tar. The caul is the membrane round the foetus in the womb; it was seen as a sign of good luck if it emerged with the baby during birth. Heaney is using the word ironically because the situation he is describing is the opposite of good luck.

tar… railings – during the Troubles in Northern Ireland Catholic women who fraternized or went out with British soldiers were stripped, had their heads shaved, were covered in tar and chained to public railing or lamp-posts – as an act of vengeance and humiliation. Tarring and feathering became a popular form of punishment in Northern Ireland, carried out by the IRA, in the 1970s. Many of the victims were women accused of conducting sexual relationships with members of the RUC or British soldiers. These terrified women had their heads shaved before being dragged to a lamppost. Once tied up, they had hot tar poured over their heads. This was followed by feathers being dumped over them which would stick to the tar for days, acting as a reminder of their so-called crimes against their community.

connive – tacitly consent to a wrong; ignore, turn a blind eye to.

Who? Heaney addresses his poem to the preserved corpse of a young woman found perfectly preserved in the peat bogs of western Denmark.

Where? Jutland, Denmark, and Northern Ireland in the last two stanzas.

When? The poem was published in 1975.

What? Heaney reflects on the preserved corpse of the young woman and links what happened to her to the treatment of Catholic women in Northern Ireland during the Troubles of the 1970s and 80s.

Commentary

The poem consists of eleven stanzas of four short lines which do not rhyme. Most lines contain two or three stressed syllables. It is not an expansive poem but very constricted and restrained – just as the young woman's corpse was constricted for centuries in the peat bog and just as Heaney's feelings (as we shall see) are constricted and restrained in his attitude to her and the Irish women who appear in the final two stanzas. The poem is divided into two halves: the first five and a half verses describe the young woman, whose body has been perfectly preserved in the peat bog, and then, half-way through stanza six, Heaney addresses the woman directly and explains his feelings towards her.

The first words of the poem *I can feel* summarize Heaney's attitude in the opening half of the poem: he feels empathy for this long-dead woman. When he addresses her in line 23 he calls her *Little adulteress* and there are signs on her corpse that she has been a victim of a ritual killing: *the halter at the nape / of her neck*, *the weighing stone*, *her shaved head*, the *blindfold* and the *noose*. Heaney assumes she was guilty of adultery. There is some question over how she died – was she hanged (*her noose*) or was she buried alive in the peat bog (*the weighing stone*) to drown. There are, however, hints of eroticism in the first half of the poem:

... the wind

on her naked front.

It blows her nipples

to amber beads.

She is slim like a sapling and her noose is described as

... a ring

to store

the memories of love —

a love deemed unacceptable by her society.

Centuries in the peat bog have left her body and hair black — the colour of peat, but in the seventh stanza Heaney imagines her when she was alive — *flaxen-haired* and *beautiful*. He admits

My poor scapegoat,

I almost love you.

However, he goes on to admit that *he would have cast, I know, / the stones of silence.* Despite almost loving her, he would not have protested at her ritual execution: he would have remained silent and not spoken up for the young woman or opposed her barbaric punishment. Heaney uses the metaphor of the stones, because in the Bible and the Koran the traditional punishment for adultery was being stoned to death: his silence would have been like a stone condemning her to death. Heaney calls himself an *artful voyeur* — fascinated by the woman and her beauty, but too ambivalent to condemn her treatment.

The final two stanzas of the poem move to contemporary Northern Ireland and Heaney writes about Catholic women who have been consorting with British soldiers and the punishment they received of being tarred and feathered and then being chained to railings or lamp-posts as a very public form of revenge and retribution. The Irish women are called the peat bog woman's *betraying sisters* and, just as he would have remained silent at the peat woman's execution, Heaney admits that he has *stood dumb*, not condemning the tarring and feathering.

In the final stanza he says he would *connive / in civilized outrage* – meaning that he would be outraged and shocked at the barbaric treatment of the women, but that he would also understand

> *... the exact*

And tribal, intimate revenge.

In conclusion, therefore, we can say that in the poem Heaney sees the acts of violence against women barbaric and cruel, but that he understands the necessity for them. He juxtaposes the values of civilization (civilized outrage) against the values of the tribe, the society, and positions himself in the middle.

In the poem the peat woman is executed as punishment; the Irish women are punished by being tarred and feathered; Heaney's 'punishment' is to be torn between civilized values and barbarity.

Conflict

The adultery of the woman in the peat bog and the tarring and feathering of the Irish girls in the final two stanzas are sources of conflict, because, in both cases, they transgressed the rules or mores of their societies. However, the real conflict is within the poet himself who feels compassion for all the women, but who understands why they were punished, and who seems to disapprove of the punishments but who says nothing. Moreover, at a deeper level it is a conflict between civilisation and more primitive tribal loyalties – which continue to exist in the modern world.

Why?

In 'Punishment' Heaney:

- takes his inspiration from the preserved corpse of a young woman found in a peat bog in Jutland, Denmark, but relates the poem to events in Northern Ireland during the Troubles.

- speculates that the young woman found in the peat bog was executed for adultery.

- generally uses short, simple language especially in the first part of the poem.

- explores his own attitude to the tarring and feathering of Northern Irish women – which is one of ambivalence.

- In a sense, condemns himself by being torn between civilised values and tribal loyalties – he feels compassion for the women but does not condemn the punishment they suffer.

'Flag' – John Agard

Author & Context

John Agard was born in the former British colony of Guyana in 1949 and he has written many books for children and adults. He moved to Britain in 1977 and lives in Sussex with his partner Grace Nichols – who is also a poet. There are other poems by Agard and Nichols in the Anthology. Agard is well-known as a skilled and adept performer of his own poems and you may get the chance to see him perform his poems during your course. You should check out his performance of the poem 'Half-Caste' on YouTube, because his performance helps to bring the poem alive. In many of his poems he uses Caribbean accent and dialect to bring a Guyanese identity to his work, but he also uses Standard English in some poems – as he does in this one.

This poem appears in a collection entitled *Half Caste and Other Poems* published in 2005. Many of the poems are concerned with race and cultural identity as well as politics and relationships.

Flags are potent symbols of a nation. For example, in the USA schoolchildren every morning in school pledge an oath of allegiance to the flag; when something controversial happens in the world, protestors often burn the flag of the country they are protesting about; when flags are run up flagpoles, people have a tendency to salute them.

Who? The poet speaks as himself. He refers to the reader in line 14 as *my friend*.

When? No specific time – this poem has a timeless quality.

Where? No specific place – it has a universal relevance.

What? A series of questions are asked and answered.

Commentary

This poem's structure is a model of simplicity and economy. Each stanza is three lines long. The first line of each stanza is a question which begins with the same words, and is followed by a two line sentence which answers the question. The second line of each stanza remains the same. The first and third lines rhyme. As in many other poems in the Anthology, the pattern the poet creates is then broken in the final stanza – by breaking the pattern the poet draws attention to the final stanza: it is fore-grounded because it breaks the pattern. In the final stanza the opening question is worded slightly differently; it is followed by two separate sentences, not one, and the second and third lines rhyme. The title of the poem is referred to implicitly in each stanza, but the word *flag* is not used in the poem until the final stanza. In addition, in the final line of each stanza Agard always uses alliteration, consonance or assonance to make the line memorable and to foreground it: *nation/knees; guts/grow; grow/bold; dares/coward; blood/bleed* – and the consonance on *l* in line 12.

Until the final stanza Agard refers to the flag dismissively and contemptuously as *just a piece of cloth*. But this piece of cloth can have remarkable powers over people:

- In the first stanza the piece of cloth *brings a nation to its knees* – an entire population falls down to worship the flag and perhaps go to war in its name.

- In the second stanza the cloth makes men brave.

- In the third stanza the power of the piece of cloth makes cowards *relent* and change – presumably to become courageous.

- In the fourth stanza Agard addresses the reader and reminds us of the consequences of war. The flag will *outlive the blood you bleed*.

- The final stanza, as we have already noticed above, changes its structure and also provides a different perspective on the flag. The opening line seems to be spoken by an imaginary reader. In the second line Agard answers the reader and reveals that the piece of cloth is just a flag. Unlike all the other stanzas here the second line does not run on into the last line — it comes to an abrupt end, before Agard delivers the final line:

Then blind your conscience to the end.

Patriotism, Agard is suggesting, allows human beings to behave in ways that allow them to ignore their conscience and to do terrible things in the name of loyalty to their country, represented by the flag.

Why?

This simply-constructed, but very powerful poem

- mocks and satirises patriotism.

- questions our loyalty to our country, any country.

- hints at the terrible, cruel and immoral things that can happen in wars.

- shows that our moral conscience might be in conflict with our patriotism.

'Phrase Book' – Jo Shapcott

Author & Context

Jo Shapcott FRSL, (born 24 March 1953, London) is an English poet, editor and lecturer who has won the National Poetry Competition, the Commonwealth Poetry Prize, the Costa Book of the Year Award, a Forward Poetry Prize and the Cholmondeley Award. Shapcott lived in Hemel Hempstead and attended Cavendish School in the town prior to studying as an undergraduate at Trinity College, Dublin. Later she studied at St Hilda's College, Oxford and received a Harkness Fellowship to Harvard. She teaches on the MA in Creative Writing at Royal Holloway, University of London. She was a Visiting Professor at the School of English Literature, Language and Linguistics, Newcastle University, was a Visiting Professor at the London Institute and was Royal Literary Fund Fellow at Oxford Brookes University from 2003-2005. She is President of the Poetry Society and is a longstanding tutor for the Arvon Foundation.

Shapcott was appointed as CBE in 2002. She initially accepted the honour but decided to refuse during the period when the British government made preparations to invade Iraq. She wrote to the Cabinet Office saying " I can't possibly accept this." She commented, "I was being diagnosed and treated for cancer, so great public statements weren't on the cards really. I was just too ill."

The First Gulf War

The Gulf War (2 August 1990 – 28 February 1991), codenamed Operation Desert Shield (2 August 1990 – 17 January 1991), for operations leading to the buildup of troops and defence of Saudi Arabia and Operation Desert Storm (17 January 1991 – 28 February 1991) in its combat phase, was a war waged by coalition forces from 34 nations led by the United States against Iraq in response to Iraq's invasion and annexation of Kuwait. In purely military terms the war was a success the Iraqis being forced to give up Kuwait. In human and environmental terms, however, the war was a disaster.

Phrases are taken from the technology of warfare circa 1991:

Human Remains Pouch - Body Bag or a bag for putting what remains of a body in.

BLISS - an acronym taught to pilots to help them remember how to evade enemy radar (the words BLISS stands for are listed in the poem); the word 'bliss' means intense pleasure which makes the word's ordinary meaning totally at odds with its meaning as a military acronym.

SLAR or Side-Looking Airborne Radar - a form of military radar.

J-Stars - Joint Surveillance Target Attack Radar System.

Kill Box - the target area for weapons fire.

Stealthed, Cleansed, Taken Out - euphemisms for killing people.

Pinpoint Accuracy - precise aim at a target (the claim that pinpoint accuracy was possible was certainly overestimated in 1991).

Harms - High-speed Anti-Radiation Missiles.

Who? The speaker, apparently a woman, watches television in her front room.

When? During the First Gulf War. The poem was first published in 1991.

Where? In the speaker's home apparently.

What? The speaker is in a state of confusion and disorientation, brought about partly by the use of military jargon which is generally euphemistic – they seek to cover the reality of war and conflict by distorting language.

Commentary

This is a confused, disorientating and fragmentary poem – and appropriately so, since this reflects the speaker's feelings and state of mind. The distortion of language seen in Shapcott's use of military jargon extends to all language in the poem, as the speaker wonders which events are true and which are false. The poem is not a realistic narrative, but a confused and seemingly random series of impressions. It represents the fragmentary experience of the world that the speaker experiences with information entering our brains from widely different sources. The language used is sometimes contradictory and by the end breaks down into short, staccato questions, whose meaning is unclear.

The poem has visual coherence – it is set out as nine four line stanzas with lines of roughly equal length, but there is no use of rhyme or rhythmic patterning – which is appropriate given the confused voice of the narrator.

The title of the poem – 'Phrase Book' – is crucial to the poem too. There are times when one might feel the need for a phrase book to understand the military jargon used by the military during a wat. Shapcott takes this idea one stage further and at times imagines she is in a foreign country where she cannot speak the language and no-one speaks English: hence her use at points of very simple sentences such as one might find in a simple phrase book. The speaker is struggling to understand what is going on in the war which is being televised and struggling to understand what is going on in her own life. This brings another aspect into the poem – love.

The random, chaotic events of the war and its language become conflated with the speaker's love life. The poem seems to question whether love is possible while war is taking place no matter how distant the war is. By the end of the poem, it could be argued that she starts to feel that war and conflict, and the difficulty of communication destroy the potential for love.

The poem begins in quite a jocular fashion, satirising military jargon:

I'm standing here inside my skin,

which will do for a Human Remains Pouch

for the moment.

But this is immediately followed by contradictory imperatives:

Look down there (up here).

Quickly. Slowly.

These contradictory imperatives reflect the confused, chaotic nature of warfare as it is experienced via television and the sheer difficulty of making sense of footage released by the military authorities of bombings and similar acts.

At the start of the second stanza Shapcott admits *I'm lost in the action, live from a war, / on screen. Lost in the action* can, of course, mean engrossed in the action, but might also imply confusion and bewilderment at what is going on. It probably means both. She then switches to phrase book mode with short sentences convey contradictory information and which serve to confuse even further:

I am Englishwoman, I don't understand you.

What's the matter? You are right. You are wrong.

Things are going well (badly). Am I disturbing you?

Wars are chaotic and confusing and whether things are going well or badly depends which side you are on. Also both sides often make contradictory claims about what has happened. The poem should be disturbing the reader at this point because of its strange and unexpected use of language.

The third stanza still focuses on the TV where the military acronym BLISS is explained, but this causes further 'phrase book' confusion – *(Please write it down. Please speak slowly).* The word *bliss* reminds the speaker of a sexual encounter in her front room:

Bliss is how it was in this very room

when I raised my body to his mouth,

when he even balanced me in the air,

or at least I thought so....

However, at this point the poem's tone becomes paranoid as the speaker imagines that the pilots can see what she and her lover are doing with their sophisticated radar systems. She seems to be convinced that she is undergoing surveillance. The rest of stanza five combines 'phrase book' with an element of sexual fantasy:

I am expecting a gentleman (a young gentleman),

two gentlemen, some gentlemen). Please send him

(them) up at once. This is really beautiful.

However, the mood changes abruptly in the sixth stanza as the speaker believes she and her lovers are being tracked by the pilot's radar (*Yes they have seen us, the pilots in the Kill Box / on their screens*) and plan to kill them:

… Stealthed, that is, Cleaned, to you and me,

Taken out. They know how to move into a single room

like that, to send in with Pinpoint Accuracy, a hundred Harms.

The speaker then transforms herself into a refugee with luggage ready to flee the imagined attack on her house: *I have two cases and a cardboard box. There is another / bag there.* In despair at the end of the stanza she asks: *Have I done enough?*

The eighth stanza starts with a simple statement: *Bliss the pilots say is for evasion and escape.* The poet goes on to ask:

What's love in all this debris?

Just one person pounding another into dust,

Into dust. I do not know the word for it yet.

The repetition of *into dust* serves to make war seem especially futile and barbaric. *I do not know the word for it yet* reminds us of the poem's title and the idea that Shapcott is having to learn a new language to understand what is going on in the war and, perhaps, a new language to understand love. She seems to be asking whether love is possible during a war or whether something so personal and intimate can exist in the face of such world-changing events as war – especially a war which mutilates language with all its euphemistic acronyms.

The final stanza breaks down into feelings of panic, guilt and paranoia with its short, staccato sentences and tone of uncertainty. It is worth quoting in full:

Where is the British Consulate? Please explain.

What does it mean? What must I do? Where

can I find? What have I done? I have done

nothing. Let me pass please. I am an Englishwoman.

The question about the British Consulate suggests she is abroad and the other questions suggest total confusion on the speaker's part – including one incomplete sentence *Where can I find?* She also seems to have been accused of some wrong-doing: *What have I done?* As a final stanza it is a superb ending to a poem full of guilt, confusion and paranoia, and ends with the one thing that Shapcott can be sure of amidst all the chaos and confusion: *I am an Englishwoman.*

Conflict

The starting point of the poem is the First Gulf War – a man-made conflict – but there are several sources of conflict in the poem. The main source of conflict is within the speaker herself, but there are good reasons for this. She struggles to make sense of the television coverage of the war and this is not helped by the manipulation of language by the military – almost a deliberate attempt to trick civilians by impressing them with jargon. The speaker experiences great conflict in trying to communicate – hence the simple sentences such as one might find in a phrase book. She is also struggling with ideas of love –

perhaps a memory of a romantic encounter or thoughts of future ones, and seems to begin to doubt that real love can exist in a world dominated by war and in which language is so debased. The location seems to change too as does her status: the poem starts in her front room but moves upstairs to the bedroom, and at one stage she seems to be a refugee ready to flee the war, while in the final stanza she appears to be abroad. Remember that all this confusion is deliberate: Shapcott is trying to convey the confused paranoia induced by the war and the TV coverage of it.

Why?

In this powerful and disturbing poem Shapcott:

- effectively portrays the chaos and confusion that war produces – even in those watching it on television.

- shows how language is debased and manipulated by military acronyms, so that even basic communication is threatened and difficult.

- through her choice of words and the use of 'phrase book' English conveys a state of mind in the speaker which is confused, paranoid and extremely vulnerable.

- reflects on love and whether it can survive war and the distortions of language.

'Honour Killing' – Imtiaz Dharker

Author & Context

Imtiaz Dharker was born in 1954 in Pakistan, but her parents emigrated to England and she grew up in Glasgow. As well as being a published poet, she is a successful film maker and book illustrator. Her work takes her between the UK and India, and she is very aware in her work of her own hybrid background, but sees it as a strength rather than a hindrance, a rich inheritance of different traditions which can coalesce rather than a source of conflict. Her poetry should be read with these contradictions in mind, as well as her desire to reconcile what she sees as trivial issues as race, background and religion.

Her collections of poems include 'Purdah' (Oxford University Press), 'Postcards from god', 'I speak for the devil' and 'The terrorist at my table' (all published by Penguin India and Bloodaxe Books UK), 'Leaving Fingerprints' (Bloodaxe Books UK) and 'Over the Moon' (September 2014, Bloodaxe Books UK). Recipient of the Cholmondeley Award and a Fellow of the Royal Society of Literature, her poems are on the English GCSE and A Level English syllabus, and she reads with other poets at Poetry Live! events all over the country to more than 25,000 students a year. She has had ten solo exhibitions of drawings in India, London, New York and Hong Kong. She scripts and directs films, many of them for non-government organizations in India, working in the area of shelter, education and health for women and children.

Purdah

Purdah or pardah is a religious and social practice of female seclusion prevalent among some Muslim communities in South Asia. The variation of purdah worn by Hindu women is known as Ghoonghat. It takes two forms: physical segregation of the sexes and the requirement that women cover their bodies so as to cover their skin and conceal their form. A woman who practices purdah can be referred to as pardanashin or purdahnishan.

Physical segregation within buildings is achieved with judicious use of walls, curtains, and screens. A woman's withdrawal into purdah usually restricts her personal, social and economic activities outside her home. The usual purdah garment worn is a burqa, which may or may not include ayashmak, a veil to conceal the face. The eyes may or may not be exposed.

Purdah was rigorously observed under the Taliban in Afghanistan, where women had to observe complete purdah at all times when they were in public. Only close male family members and other women were allowed to see them out of purdah. In other societies, purdah is often only practised during certain times of religious significance.

Honour Killing

An honor killing or shame killing is the homicide of a member of a family by other members, due to the perpetrators' belief that the victim has brought shame or dishonor upon the family, or has violated the principles of a community or a religion, usually for reasons such as refusing to enter an arranged marriage, being in a relationship that is disapproved of by their family, having sex outside marriage, becoming the victim of rape, dressing in ways which are deemed inappropriate, engaging in non-heterosexual relations or renouncing a faith The distinctive nature of honor killings is the collective nature of the crime - many members of an extended family plan the act together, sometimes through a formal "family council". Another significant feature is the connection of honor killings to the control of women's behaviour, in particular in regard to sexuality/male interaction/marriage, by the family as a collective. Another key aspect is the importance of the reputation of the family in the community, and the stigma associated with losing social status, particularly in tight-knit communities. Another characteristic of honor killings is that the perpetrators often don't face negative stigma within their communities, because their behaviour is seen as justified.

mangalsutra – a necklace traditionally placed around the bride's neck during a marriage service.

Who? The poet speaks as herself.

When? The present.

Where? No specific location.

What? Dharker attacks the archaic treatment of women in some Islamic societies and asserts her own independence.

Commentary

'In Lahore, in the last year of the 20th century, a woman was shot by her family in her lawyer's office. Her crime was that she had asked for a divorce. The whole Pakistan senate refused to condemn the act. They called it an 'Honour Killing.' (Dharker)

Instead of having the heart, or for that purpose even head, to condemn the killing at any level, it was welcomed as "honour killing". Imtiaz Dharker's sensitivity could not remain silent and it burst forth in her poem "Honour Killing". Its reading makes a powerful impact and it sensitises the reader, awakens and rouses his/her conscience to the urgent feminist concerns. Honour killings are known as 'karo-kari' in Pakistan and enjoy a high level of support there, despite widespread condemnation from human rights associations. The concept of women as 'property' and 'honour' is so deeply rooted in the culture of Pakistan that the state ignores the regular occurrences of women being killed by their families. It is also because the religious leaders use justifications from their religious books for sanctioning punishments against the 'disobedient' women.

In the first stanza Dharker announces that she is

... taking off this coat,

this black coat of a country

that I swore for years was mine

that I wore more out of habit

than design.

Born wearing it,

I believed I had no choice.

Pakistan is transformed into a metaphor – *this black coat of a country* – and which she believed she has no choice but to wear. Her tone is assertive and confident.

The whole poem is a rejection of the social customs and mores of Pakistan and the way women are expected to dress in a certain way. It is a poem of liberation which asserts that Dharker does have a choice over what she wears and the woman she becomes.

The second stanza continues in this manner: *I'm taking off this veil.* She points out that it is the

... black veil of a faith

that made me faithless

to myself.

By making it faithless to herself she is forced into being someone she is not with all her potential unfulfilled. It *tied her mouth* and *muffled [her] own voice* – forcing her to deny the woman she wanted to become. Imtiaz Dharker is a talented and creative woman and she felt constrained and oppressed by the culture she was born into, as it denied her or made difficult the fulfilment of her artistic expression and her desire to live as a modern woman – not consigned to a dress code and religious attitudes that seem, to modern eyes, medieval. She also writes that the veil *gave my god a devil's face* - thus showing her hostility towards contemporary Islam: however, it also shows what Dharker sees as the malign influence of extreme Islam and the constraints of the dress code, as well as the practice of honour killing.

In the third stanza she removes the silks she is expected to wear and all the jewellery too. She uses an interesting phrase – *dictator dreams* – making it clear that all the things she is rejecting are means of controlling women by men (who are the dictators). At the end of the stanza her rings are said to be

Rattling in a tin cup of needs

That beggared me.

Dharker has needs, but they are not fulfilled by the rings and the necklace which *beggared* her despite their monetary value – she wants to do something more meaningful with her life, than simply be a wife and mother hidden behind a veil.

In the fourth stanza she describes attempting to discover the woman she really is: she strips away her skin, her face, her flesh and her womb to reveal the real woman inside. Even the womb must go because she does not want to be judged by her gender. In the process of taking off these claims, she realized that she has choices which she had never known before when her life was restricted: *Born wearing it/ I believed I had no choice.* She removes every part of her body before creating a new geography for herself. She does not even hesitate to remove her womb as she wants to be free from any kind of restriction which could be placed on her due to her sex. *I'm taking off this skin, / and then the face the flesh, The womb.* Now when she is free from every gender restriction and religious affiliation, she demands: *Let's see/ What I am in here / When I squeeze past / The easy cage of bone.*

The fifth stanza is truly speculative and starts

Let's see

>*what I am in here*

to discover the talents that were supressed by her faith.

The final stanza represents her complete liberation from her faith and its customs:

Let's see

what I am out here

making, crafting,

plotting at my new geography.

Dharker is a highly respected poet and artist who splits her time between Scotland and Pakistan – her new geography – and she has forged a highly successful career as an independent woman who has rejected the antiquated mores of traditional Islam. Her rebellion against her culture has been successful.

So in the poem 'Honour Killing' it is not woman who is killed, but "a notion of honour that from the speaker's perspective burdens women with a life that forces them to betray and neglect themselves." (Lehmann, 2012 Online). Thus, the poem has a double meaning: as Dharker strips away the accumulated layers of herself (herself as constructed by her society), so she destroys any notion that such a killing could be anything to do with honour. Although it is very dangerous to go against religious orthodoxy and face the wrath of religious leaders, Dharker doesn't fear reprisal, but presents her thoughts and emotions in a bold and candid way and even doesn't hesitate to rebel against cultural and religious orthodoxy

The poem consists of six stanzas with occasional rhyme. Essentially it is written in free verse which reflects well the freedom that Dharker achieves through writing the poem. One oddity is that the lines of each stanza are indented after the first line: this too asserts her independence especially as four of the six stanzas start (or contain in the first line) the words I'm, showing how Dharker is asserting herself against her culture.

Conflict

The conflict in the poem is between the poet and the country (Pakistan) and the faith (Islam) she is born into. More broadly, it is between her freedom to wear what she likes and do what she wants and the repressive social mores of the society she is born into – which are designed to repress women and control what they wear and what they do. The notion of honour killing is central to this oppression of the female gender under Islamic law, as are the restrictive dress codes which cover up a woman's body and her face. In the act of writing and publishing the poem Dharker proclaims her freedom from gender and religious stereotypes. The title of the poem – 'Honour Killing' – has a specific meaning, but by the end of the poem it takes on a new meaning. By stripping away all the layers of her religion's intolerance and repression of women, it is as if, metaphorically, Dharker has 'killed' her own 'honour' – an honour which she did not want and is the product of a particular society's restrictive mores. She emerges a free woman.

Why?

In 'Honour Killing' Imtiaz Dharker

- writes a passionate poem protesting about the way women are treated in some Islamic countries, especially Pakistan and in some Islamic communities outside Pakistan.

- starting with her clothes, she gradually strips away all the things that make her a woman (and, therefore, an oppressed person in her culture) to find her real self.

- writes a poem the main tone of which is anger and outrage, but which ends, in the final stanza, in an optimistic, celebratory way.

- given the current climate of extremism, writes a brave, defiant poem.

- gives the hope of change to other oppressed women.

'Partition' – Sujata Bhatt
Author & Context

Sujata Bhatt (born 6 May 1956) is an Indian poet, a native speaker of Gujarati. Sujata Bhatt was born in Ahmedabad, Gujarat and brought up in Pune until 1968, when she emigrated to United States with her family. She has an MFA from the University of Iowa, and for a time was writer-in-residence at the University of Victoria, Canada. She received the Commonwealth Poetry Prize (Asia) and the Alice Hunt Bartlett Award for her first collection *Brunizem*. She received a Cholmondeley Award in 1991 and the Italian Tratti Poetry Prize in 2000. Her translations from the German include *Mickle Makes Muckle: poems, mini plays and short prose* by Michael Augustin (Dedalus Press, 2007). Bhatt was a visiting fellow at Dickinson College, Pennsylvania and currently works as a freelance writer. She has translated Gujarati poetry into English for the *Penguin Anthology of Contemporary Indian Women Poets*. Combining Gujarati and English, Bhatt writes "Indian-English rather than Anglo-Indian poetry." Her poems have appeared in various journals in the United Kingdom, Ireland, the United States, and Canada, and have been widely anthologised, as well as being broadcast on British, German, and Dutch radio. In 2013 she was made Visiting Professor of Creative Writing at Nottingham Trent University.

Michael Schmidt observed that her "free verse is fast-moving, urgent with narratives, softly spoken. Her cadence is natural, her diction undecorated." Bhatt has been recognized as a distinctive voice in contemporary poetry. She is, the *New Statesman* declared, "one of the finest poets alive". Her poem 'A Different History' dealing with the issues of globalization and westernization, featured in the poetry anthology used for IGCSE English examinations, for examination in 2014.

Bhatt now lives in Bremen, Germany with her husband, the German writer Michael Augustin, and daughter. She is a Visiting Professor in Creative Writing at Nottingham Trent University.

The Partition of India

British India before Partition

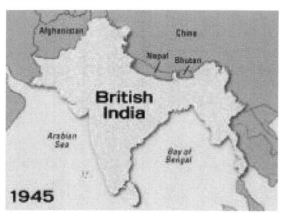

The Partition of India was the partition of the British Indian Empire[that led to the creation of the sovereign states of the Dominion of Pakistan (which later split into Pakistan and Bangladesh) and the Union of India (later the Republic of India) on 15 August 1947 at midnight. "Partition" here refers not only to the division of the Bengal province of British India into East Pakistan and West Bengal (India), and the similar partition of the Punjab Province into West Punjab (West Pakistan) and East Punjab (now Punjab), but also to the respective divisions of other assets, including the British Indian Army, the Indian Civil Service and other administrative services, the railways, and the central treasury. The reason for the partition was sectarian hostility between Muslims and Hindus. There was a massive movement of people: Muslims to West and East Pakistan; and Hindus to India. However, they did not all move to the states designated for them: millions of Hindus live in Pakistan and millions of Muslims live in India – unable or unwilling to move when Partition occurred. So sectarian violence remains today. Furthermore, there have been constant disputes over the frontier. Frequent border skirmishes and two wars, centring on the disputed province of Kashmir. Some would say partition was rushed through which exacerbated the problems and, in drawing the borders where they did, the British sowed the seeds of conflict between the newly created nations.

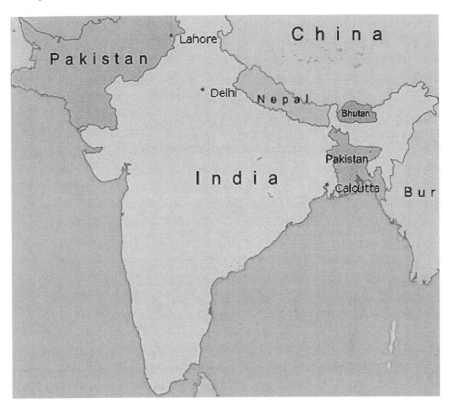

British India after partition

In the riots which preceded the partition in the Punjab Province, it is believed that between 200,000 and 2,000,000 people were killed in the retributive genocide between the religions. UNHCR estimates 14 million Hindus, Sikhs and Muslims were displaced during the partition; it was the largest mass migration in human history and a deeply traumatic event in the life of the area.

Ahmedabad – also known as Amdavad is the largest city and former capital of Gujarat, which is a state in India. It is the administrative headquarters of the Ahmedabad district and the seat of the Gujarat High Court. With a population of more than 6.3 million and an extended population of 7.2 million, it is the sixth largest city and seventh largest metropolitan area of India. Ahmedabad is located on the banks of the Sabarmati River, 30 km (19 miles) from the state capital Gandhinagar.

neem trees – trees the products of which have been used in India for centuries for medicinal purposes.

Who? The speaker relates her mother and her great-aunt's experiences of partition in 1997 (*when India / is fifty*), but looking back decades.

When? In 1947 – the year India was partitioned.

Where? Near Ahmedabad railway station.

What? The speaker's mother goes every day to take food and water to the people at the railway station and reflects on Partition.

Commentary

This is a very personal and intimate poem about a huge historical event. It is written in free verse – a mode of writing often favoured by post-colonial writers who want to reject traditional European forms of verse which involve rhyme or any strict pattern.

The opening sentence relates how the poet's mother was nineteen when Partition took place

and when she stood in her garden

she could hear the cries of the people

stranded in the Ahmedabad railway station.

The huge numbers of people are suggested by the mother feeling the sound was endless.

Her mother's aunt would go every day to the railway station with food and water for the people stranded there, but her mother

... felt afraid,

felt she could not go with her aunt —

So she stood in the garden

listening.

The far-reaching changes that Partition will bring are hinted at because *Even the birds sounded different — / and the shadows cast by the neem trees / brought no consolation.* The mother desperately wants to go with her aunt to help the poor people at the station, but fear holds her back.

In line 20 we suddenly are brought up to 1997 and 50th anniversary of Partition and India's independence from British rule. Of course, as the mother says *India is older than that.... India was always there.* They are talking at midnight — the exact moment fifty years earlier that India gained her independence. The mother admits that she still feels guilty about not helping by going with her aunt to the railway station.

The poem ends with a rhetorical question about partition. It is said in an almost jocular fashion, but coming so soon after the mother admitting her lasting sense of guilt, it hints that the British should still feel guilty about how they handled and rushed Partition through:

How could they

> *have let a man*

who knew nothing

> *about geography*

divide a country?

There is bitterness and deep sadness in this question too, given the appalling suffering that Partition caused – both for those who died and those whose lives were uprooted by being forced to move. The overall tone of the poem is sadness and regret – the personal regret of the mother who was afraid to go to the railway station and the deeper, wider regret over Partition. Bhatt gives the poem an intimate tone by focusing on the feelings of her mother.

Conflict

The main conflict is caused by the Partition of India which is criticised in the final sentence of the poem. Within the poem, however, Partition is only seen or rather heard through the masses of people crying at the nearby railway station. The real conflict in the poem concerns the speaker's mother who wanted to go to the railway station but was too afraid. In the mother's fear Bhatt uses a very personal and intimate experience to try to summarize the manifold fears that Partition caused, and the people stranded at the railway station are a small part of the suffering British India and its inhabitants suffered.

Why?

In 'Partition' Bhatt:

- chooses to deal with an enormous historical event in a small-scale intimate way.

- uses the mother's fear to summarise succinctly the tremendous trauma that Partition caused.

- conveys well the mother's distress at the situation.

- uses a calm and stoical tone until the final question which scathingly condemns the British handling of Partition.

Glossary

The Oxford Concise Dictionary of Literary Terms has been invaluable in writing this section of the book. I would again remind the reader that knowledge of these terms is only the start – do NOT define a word you find here in the examination. You can take it for granted that the examiner knows the term: it is up to you to try to use it confidently and with precision and to explain why the poet uses it or what effect it has on the reader.

ALLITERATION   the repetition of the same sounds – usually initial consonants or stressed syllables – in any sequence of closely adjacent words.

ALLUSION   an indirect or passing reference to some event, person, place or artistic work which is not explained by the writer, but which relies on the reader's familiarity with it.

AMBIGUITY   openness to different interpretations.

ANAPAEST   a metrical foot made up of two unstressed syllables followed by a stressed syllable.

ANAPHORA the repetition of a word or a phrase at the start of consecutive lines of poetry, or clauses, or sentences.

ASSONANCE the repetition of similar vowel sounds in neighbouring words.

BALLAD   a folk song or orally transmitted poem telling in a simple and direct way a story with a tragic ending. Ballads are normally composed in quatrains with the second and fourth lines rhyming. Such quatrains are known as the ballad stanza because of its frequent use in what we call ballads.

BLANK VERSE   unrhymed lines of ten syllable length. This is a widely used form by Shakespeare in his plays, by Milton and by

Wordsworth.

CAESURA　any pause in a line of verse caused by punctuation. This can draw attention to what precedes or follows the caesura and also, by breaking up the rhythm of the line, can slow the poem down and make it more like ordinary speech.

CANON　a body of writings recognized by authority. The canon of a national literature is a body of writings especially approved by critics or anthologists and deemed suitable for academic study. Towards the end of the 20th century there was a general feeling that the canon of English Literature was dominated by dead white men and since then there has been a deliberate and fruitful attempt made to give more prominence to writing by women and by writers from non-white backgrounds. Even your Anthology is a contribution to the canon, because someone sat down and decided that the poems included in it were worthy of study by students taking GCSE.

CARPE DIEM　a Latin phrase from the Roman poet Horace which means 'seize the day' – 'make the best of the present moment'. It is a very common theme of European lyric poetry, in which the speaker of a poem argues that since time is short and death is inevitable, pleasure should be enjoyed while there is still time.

COLLOCATION　the act of putting two words together. What this means in practice is that certain words have very common collocations – in other words they are usually found in written or spoken English in collocation with other words. For example, the word *Christmas* is often collocated with words such as *cards, presents, carols, holidays,* but you won't often find it collocated with *sadness.* This can be an important term because poets, who are seeking to use words in original ways, will often put two words together which are not often collocated.

COLLOQUIALISM　the use of informal expressions or vocabulary appropriate to everyday speech rather than the formality of writing. When used in poetry it can make the poem seem more down-to-earth and real, more honest and intimate.

CONCEIT   an unusually far-fetched metaphor presenting a surprising and witty parallel between two apparently dissimilar things or feelings.

CONSONANCE   the repetition of identical or similar consonants in neighbouring words whose vowel sounds are different.

CONTEXT   the biographical, social, cultural and historical circumstances in which a text is produced and read and understood – you might to like to think of it as its background. However, it is important sometimes to consider the reader's own context – especially when we look back at poems from the Literary Heritage. To interpret a poem with full regard to its background is to contextualize it.

COUPLET   a pair of rhyming verse lines, usually of the same length.

CROSSED RHYME   the rhyming of one word in the middle of a long line of poetry with a word in a similar position in the next line.

DACTYL   a metrical foot having two unstressed syllables followed by a stressed syllable.

DIALECT   a distinctive variety of language, spoken by members of an identifiable regional group, nation or social class. Dialects differ from one another in pronunciation, vocabulary and grammar. Traditionally they have been looked down on and viewed as variations from an educated 'standard' form of the language, but linguists point out that standard forms themselves are merely dialects which have come to dominate for social and political reasons. In English this notion of dialect is especially important because English is spoken all over the world and there are variations between the English spoken in, say, Yorkshire, Delhi and Australia. Dialects now are increasingly celebrated as a distinct way of speaking and writing which are integral to our identity.

DICTION   the choice of words used in any literary work.

DISSONANCE   harshness of sound.

DRAMATIC MONOLOGUE   a kind of poem in which a single fictional or historical character (not the poet) speaks to a silent audience and unwittingly reveals the truth about their character.

ELEGY   a lyric poem lamenting the death of a friend or public figure or reflecting seriously on a serious subject. The elegiac has come to refer to the mournful mood of such poems.

ELLIPSIS   the omission from a sentence of a word or words which would be required for complete clarity. It is used all the time in everyday speech, but is often used in poetry to promote compression and/or ambiguity. The adjective is elliptical.

END-RHYME   rhyme occurring at the end of a line of poetry. The most common form of rhyme.

END-STOPPED   a line of poetry brought to a pause by the use of punctuation. The opposite of enjambment.

ENJAMBMENT   caused by the lack of punctuation at the end of a line of poetry, this causes the sense (and the voice when the poem is read aloud) to 'run over' into the next line. In general, this can impart to poems the feel of ordinary speech, but there are examples in the Anthology of more precise reasons for the poet to use enjambment.

EPIPHANY   a sudden moment of insight or revelation, usually at   the end of a poem.

EPIZEUXIS   the technique by which a word is repeated for emphasis with no other words intervening

EUPHONY   a pleasing smoothness of sound

FALLING RHTHYM   a rhythmical effect in which the end of the lines of a poem consist of trochees or dactyls. The effect is often of uncertainty or poignancy, but it can also be used for comic effect.

FEMININE ENDING   any line of poetry which ends on an unstressed   syllable and which ensures the line ends on a falling rhythm.

FIGURATIVE   Not literal. Obviously 'figurative' language covers metaphor and simile and personification

FIGURE OF SPEECH   any expression which departs from the ordinary literal sense or normal order of words. Figurative language (the opposite of literal language) includes metaphor, simile and personification. Some figures of speech – such as alliteration and assonance achieve their effects through the repetition of sounds.

FOREGROUNDING giving unusual prominence to one part of a text. Poetry differs from everyday speech and prose by its use of regular rhythm, metaphors, alliteration and other devices by which its language draws attention to itself.

FREE VERSE a kind of poetry that does not conform to any regular pattern of line length or rhyme. The length of its lines are irregular as is its use of rhyme – if any.

HALF-RHYME   an imperfect rhyme – also known as para-rhyme, near rhyme and slant rhyme – in which the final consonants match but the vowel sounds do not match. Pioneered in the 19th century by the poets Emily Dickinson and Gerard Manley Hopkins, and made even more popular by Wilfred Owen and T S Eliot in the early 20th century,

HOMONYM   a word that is identical to another word either in sound or in spelling

HOMOPHONE   a word that is pronounced in the same way as another word but which differs in meaning and/or spelling.

HYPERBOLE exaggeration for the sake of emphasis.

IAMB a metrical foot of verse having one stressed syllable followed by one unstressed. Lines made up predominately of iambs are referred to as iambics or iambic verse. The 10 syllable iambic pentameter (rhymed or unrhymed) is the most common line in English poetry. The 8 syllable iambic tetrameter is also very popular. The 12 syllable iambic hexameter is less common in English and is also known as the alexandrine. Even if the rhythm of a poem is predominately iambic, it does not preclude metrical variation – often with a trochaic foot at the start of a line to give maximum impact.

IDIOM an everyday phrase that cannot be translated literally because its meaning does not correspond to the specific words in the phrase. There are thousands in English like – *you get up my nose, when pigs fly, she was all ears*.

IMAGERY a rather vague critical term covering literal and metaphorical language which evoke sense impressions with reference to concrete objects – the things the writer describes.

INTERNAL RHYME a poetic device in which two or more words in the same line rhyme.

INTERTEXTUALITY the relationship that a text may have with another preceding and usually well-known text.

INVERSION the reversal of the normally-expected order of words. 'Normally expected' means how we might say the words in the order of normal speech; to invert the normal word order usually draws attention or foregrounds the words.

JUXTAPOSITION two things that are placed alongside each other.

LAMENT any poem expressing profound grief usually in the face of death.

LATINATE   Latinate diction in English means the use of words derived from Latin rather than those derived from Old English.

LITOTES   understatement – the opposite of hyperbole.

LYRIC   any fairly short poem expressing the personal mood of the speaker.

MASCULINE ENDING   Any line of poetry which ends on a stressed syllable.

METAPHOR   the most important figure of speech in which in which one thing is referred to by a word normally associated with another thing, so as to suggest some common quality shared by both things. In metaphor, this similarity is directly stated, unlike in a simile where the resemblance is indirect and introduced by the words like or as. Much of our everyday language is made up of metaphor too – to say someone is as greedy as a pig is a simile; to say he is a pig is a metaphor.

MNEMONIC   a form of words or letters that helps people remember things. It is common in everyday sayings and uses some of the features of language that we associate with poetry. For example, the weather saying Red sky at night, shepherd's delight uses rhyme.

MONOLOGUE`   an extended speech uttered by one speaker.

NARRATOR   the one who tells or is assumed to be the voice of the poem.

OCTAVE or OCTET a group of eight lines forming the first part of a sonnet.

ONOMATOPOEIA the use of words that seem to imitate the sounds they refer to (*bang*, *whizz*, *crackle*, *fizz*) or any combination or words in which the sound echoes or seems to echo the sense. The adjective is onomatopoeic, so you can say that *blast* is an onomatopoeic word.

ORAL TRADITION the passing on from one generation to another of songs, chants, poems, proverbs by word of mouth and memory.

OXYMORON   a figure of speech that combines two seemingly contradictory terms as in the everyday terms bitter-sweet and living-death.

PARALLELISM   the arrangement of similarly constructed clause, sentences or lines of poetry.

PARADOX   a statement which is self-contradictory.

PATHETIC FALLACY   this is the convention that natural phenomena (usually the weather) are a reflection of the poet's or the narrator's mood. It may well involve the personification of things in nature, but does not have to. At its simplest, a writer might choose to associate very bad weather with a mood of depression and sadness.

PERSONA   the assumed identity or fictional narrator assumed by a writer.

PERSONIFICATIONa figure of speech in which animals, abstract ideas or lifeless things are referred to as if they were human. Sometimes known as personal metaphor.

PETRARCHAN   characteristic of the Italian poet Petrarch (1304 – 1374). Mainly applied to the Petrarchan sonnet which is different in its form from the Shakespearean sonnet.

PHONETIC SPELLING   a technique writers use which involves misspelling a word in order to imitate the accent in which the word is said.

PLOSIVE   explosive. Used to describe sounds that we form by putting our lips together such as *b* and *p*.

POSTCOLONIAL LITERATURE a term devised to describe what used to be called Commonwealth Literature (and before that Empire Writing!). The term covers a very wide range of writing from countries that were once colonies of European countries. It has come to include some writing by writers of non-white racial backgrounds whose roots or family originated in former colonies – no matter where they live now.

PUN an expression that derives humour either through using a word that has two distinct meanings or two similar sounding words (homophones).

QUATRAIN a verse stanza of four lines – usually rhymed.

REFRAIN a line, or a group of lines, repeated at intervals throughout a poem – usually at regular intervals and at the end of a stanza.

RHYME the identity of sound between syllables or paired groups of syllables usually at the end of a line of poetry.

RHYME SCHEME the pattern in which the rhymed line endings are arranged in any poem or stanza. This is normally written as a sequence of letters where each line ending in the same rhyme is given the same alphabetical letter. So a Shakespearean sonnet's rhyme scheme is ababcdcdefefgg, but the rhyme scheme of a Petrarchan sonnet is abbaabbacdecde. In other poems the rhyme scheme might be arranged to suit the poet's convenience or intentions. For example, in Blake's 'London' the first stanza rhymes abab, the second cdcd and so on.

RHYTHM a pattern of sounds which is repeated with the stress falling on the same syllables (more or less) in each line. However, variations to the pattern, especially towards the end of the poem, often stand out and are foregrounded because they break the pattern the poet has built up through the course of the poem.

ROMANTICISM the name given to the artistic movement that emerged in England and Germany in the 1790s and in the rest of Europe in the 1820s and beyond. It was a movement that saw great changes in literature, painting, sculpture, architecture and music and found its catalyst in the new philosophical ideas of Jean Jacques Rousseau and Thomas Paine, and in response to the French and industrial revolutions. Its chief emphasis was on freedom of individual self-expression, sincerity, spontaneity and originality, but it also looked to the distant past of the Middle Ages for some of its inspiration.

SATIRE   any type of writing which exposes and mocks the foolishness or evil of individuals, institutions or societies. A poem can be satiric (adjective) or you can say a poet satirizes something or somebody.

SESTET   a group of six lines forming the second half of a sonnet, following the octet.

SIBILANCE   the noticeable recurrence of *s* sounds.

SIMILE   an explicit comparison between two different things, actions or feelings, usually introduced by *like* or *as*.

SONNET   a lyric poem of 14 lines of equal length. The form originated in Italy and was made famous as a vehicle for love poetry by Petrarch and came to be adopted throughout Europe. The standard subject matter of early sonnets was romantic love, but in the 17th century John Donne used it to write religious poetry and John Milton wrote political sonnets, so it came to be used for any subject matter. The sonnet form enjoyed a revival in the Romantic period (Wordsworth, Keats and Shelley all wrote them) and continues to be widely used today. Some poets have written connected series of sonnets and these are known as sonnet cycles. Petrarchan sonnets differ slightly in their rhyme scheme from Shakespearean sonnets (see the entry above on rhyme scheme). A Petrarchan sonnet consists of two quatrains (the octet) followed by two tercets (the sestet). A Shakespearean sonnet consists of two quatrains (the octet) followed by another quatrain and a final couplet (the sestet).

SPONDEE   a metrical unit consisting of two stressed syllables.

STANZA   a group of verse lines forming a section of a poem and sharing the same structure in terms of the length of the lines, the rhyme scheme and the rhythm.

STYLE   any specific way of using language, which is characteristic of an author, a period, a type of poetry or a group of writers.

SYLLOGISM   a form of logical argument that draws a conclusion from two propositions.

SYMBOL   anything that represents something else. A national flag symbolizes the country that uses it; symbols are heavily used in road signs. In poetry symbols can represent almost anything. Blake's 'The Sick Rose' is a good example of a poem which uses a symbol.

SYNECDOCHE   a figure of speech in which a thing or person is referred to indirectly, either by naming some part of it (*hands* for manual labourers) or by naming some big thing of which it is a part (the law for police officers). As you can see from these examples, it is a common practice in speech.

TONE   a critical term meaning the mood or atmosphere of a piece of writing. It may also include the sense of the writer's attitude to the reader of the subject matter.

TROCHEE   a metrical foot having a stressed syllable followed by an unstressed syllable.

TURN   the English term for a sudden change in mood or line of argument, especially in line 9 of a sonnet.

VERSE   another word for poetry as opposed to prose.

The use of the word 'verse' sometimes implies writing that rhymes and has a rhythm, but perhaps lacks the merit of real poetry.

VERSE PARAGRAPH   a group of lines of poetry forming a section of a poem, the length of the unit being determined by the sense rather than a particular stanza pattern.

VOLTA   the Italian term for the 'turn' in the argument or mood of a sonnet which normally occurs in the ninth line at the start of the sestet, but sometimes in Shakespearean sonnets is delayed until the final couplet.

WIT   a general term which covers the idea of intelligence, but refers in poetry more specifically to verbal ingenuity and cleverness.

23780621R00084

Printed in Great Britain
by Amazon